GROWING AND SELLING

# A SUCCESSFUL CONSULTING FIRM

3E PUBLISHING | LONDON | SYDNEY |

GROWING AND SELLING A
SUCCESSFUL CONSULTING FIRM

RAJ ASEERVATHAM PhD MBA

3E PUBLISHING | LONDON | SYDNEY |

GROWING AND SELLING
A SUCCESSFUL
CONSULTING
FIRM

RAJ ASEERVATHAM PhD MBA

## CHAPTER 1: LUCRATIVE WISDOM

*In those days he was wiser than he is now. He used to frequently take my advice* – Winston Churchill

What are the types of consulting to consider for your enterprise? How do you decide between these, and what hybrids might suit you?

## CHAPTER 2: THE EXIT STRATEGY

*If you want a happy ending, that depends, of course, on where you stop your story* – Orson Welles

What does the end look like? What is the vision you want to hold firm, the one that gives you purpose, clarity and inexhaustible determination?

## CHAPTER 3: FINDING CONSULTANTS

*The best way to find yourself is to lose yourself in the service of others* – Mahatma Gandhi

Consultants come in different flavors. What are their characteristics? How do you work out what mix of flavors you need for your enterprise?

## CHAPTER 4: KEEPING CONSULTANTS

*It is best not to swap horses when crossing the river* – Abraham Lincoln

If the best consultants are ego-driven performers and everyone wants them, how do you think about the culture you must foster to keep them loyal to you?

## CHAPTER 5: DOING WHAT YOU DO

*Choose a job you love and you will never have to work a day in your life* - Confucius

On this journey to your vision, with an increasing number of disciples in tow, how will you keep the excitement in your staff, in your firm, and very importantly, yourself?


## CHAPTER 6: GROW WITH PURPOSE

*Do, or do not. There is no try* - Yoda

How do you create a growth engine that keeps revving; one that incentivizes your staff to strive for growth, and one that signals when and how to grow?


## CHAPTER 7: DEBT FREE GROWTH

*Money often costs too much* - Ralph Waldo Emerson

If the conventional wisdom is that growth requires borrowings, how can you manage the cashflow of your firm so that you avoid falling into debt?


## CHAPTER 8: PARTNERING

*Talent wins games, but teamwork and intelligence win championships* - Michael Jordan

If you don't want to take this journey alone, how do you approach the issue of working with others in a co-owned firm to realize your own vision?

## CHAPTER 9: STUMBLING

*I like to make my own mistakes* – Mikhael Baryshnikov

You will not put every foot right on this journey.
What can you learn about the inevitability of error?

## CHAPTER 10: EXIT

*I been a long time leaving but I'm going to
be a long time gone* – Willie Nelson

How do you execute the final moves in your strategy,
and what could it feel like for you?

# TABLE OF CONTENTS

# PREFACE

*If you've picked up this book, it's because you have an itch. You've toyed with the idea of being your own boss, running your own professional services consulting firm. Maybe you've dreamed of building a company from nothing, to something with size and value. And maybe you wonder whether this valuable asset can be sold, and for how much.*

*If you're like me, no one has taught you how to build your own firm and to sell it successfully. The task seems daunting, reserved for those people referred to as 'entrepreneurs', for which there seems no prescribed course at University.*

*While many who try to successfully grow their firms do not, some actually do, and often with stunning results. How do they do it? Do you need special training? Is it genius?*

*The answer, in my opinion, is that it does not need special training, and it's far from genius. But it does need some knowledge, some idea of the dos and don'ts, a liberal dollop of hard work, and a clear strategy.*

*There are many useful books on how to win clients and write successful proposals; I have not tried to replicate these and I encourage you to refer to them if you are starting consulting. Instead I have focused on growing an enterprise, creating value in it, and selling it, and tried to distil this into ten chapters, each dealing with a key principle. I have assumed that before you begin this challenge you are, in your own right, a capable consultant. I have not covered legal and indemnity issues, and again I have assumed you will research these things before you start your own enterprise. For this book, I have focused only on those lessons I could not find when I looked for them.*

*I've organized the lessons into the ten most useful principles that I would like to have known when I first started my own consulting enterprise. I've included many mini-case studies, which I would more accurately refer to as 'case observations'. And I have changed the names of those involved, to preserve their anonymity.*

*This book contains a growth model that is not out of a textbook, nor out of conventional practice. I developed it as a proprietary model while doing my MBA thesis, and then applied it in real life over the next decade. I personally credit it with much of the commercial success I have experienced, but I observe that it is not common wisdom, so please use it – with my blessing – with that in mind.*

*I hope this book, and the few lessons offered, help you fulfill your own dreams of growing and selling a successful consulting firm.*

*Raj Aseervatham*

# ACKNOWLEDGMENTS

*Clearly I didn't invent consulting! The successes and failures of others dwarf mine; and while the principles I espouse are the ones I live by, I did borrow many of them from others. So I must acknowledge a number of consultants, many who have successfully built their own consulting firms, some who've shared with me their greatest regrets, and others who have contributed in various ways to this book. I have borrowed liberally from their wisdom, actions and experiences; many of theirs are more compelling than my own. Paul Mitchell, Terence Jeyaretnam, Errol Briese, Serena Russo, Randal Hinz, Peter Hansen, John Alexander, Sandy Vigar, Graeme Beissel, David Shirley, Chandran Nair, Peter Ryan, Paul Gilding and Bob McCotter are consultants who just know about enterprises.*

*Victoria Jay and Toni Jordan inspired me to write down my thoughts and experiences, and to share my knowledge. They gave me the benefit of their honesty and wisdom with their insightful reviews. My father Al insisted I write, and for several decades provided an example for me to follow.*

*An army of clients, too many to recall, taught me many things about successful consulting. A smaller legion of staff in several countries, whom I'm glad to say I can remember to the last person, taught me much, much more, and helped me achieve my own visions. This book is dedicated to them.*

# CHAPTER 1
# LUCRATIVE WISDOM

*In those days he was wiser than he is now.*
*He used to frequently take my advice.*
*– Winston Churchill*

## The core of consulting

Successful consultants do well for themselves. Don't get me wrong. The average consultant is not a multi-millionaire. He or she is what you might call comfortably well off. The average consultant is probably financially better off than the average government employee. A good consultant is likely to be financially better off than if in private industry or a corporation (although it is possible to find more exceptions in this latter comparison than the previous one). But on the other side of the ledger, the average consultant foregoes the relative safety of a fixed salary every month with the more lucrative, but riskier, finances of a hand-to-mouth existence.

The average consultant swings from famine to feast in a matter of weeks, while those in government or the corporate world rarely encounter famine and – again, on average – only occasionally encounter feast!

If the average consultant's lot is not so bad – and in the eyes of some it's actually pretty attractive – then what is in store for the truly successful consultant? The answer is, *quite a bit!* It's not an easy industry, and it is cut-throat competitive, but it can be lucrative. How lucrative, you ask?

Let's talk numbers to put this in perspective, and test the paradigm of the "million-dollar consultant". Let's look at a top-notch consultant, a professional with a very good reputation, who works every day of the year, except for weekends (he or she takes no vacations), works ten hours a day (all of which he or she can bill to the client), and is able to charge $400 for every hour of his/her time. This person works 250 days per year, 10 hours per day (or 2,500 hours per year) at $400 per hour… which, if you do the math, is *voila* – a million dollars.

So it's possible. But how practical is it? Let's think about it. Where does he or she find the time to market to new clients? Maybe the weekends? Will every client pay $400 per hour? Or, put another way, is the type of consulting that our consultant practices worth $400 per hour to all their clients? What if you're a human resources consultant and you specialize in developing corporate talent? Or if you're an IT consultant specializing in office networks? Are these necessarily $400-per-hour activities? And what about work/life balance, if you happen to make the magic million-dollar equation? And how much of this million dollars is paid to the tax-man? That's a lot of questions. The term "million-dollar consultant" doesn't quite roll off the tongue now, does it?

One possibility is that the consultant offers a risk-reward contract. "I'll save you a hundred million dollars in operating costs, and my fee is one percent of what I save you." That's a million dollar fee. This is a good model, but in truth it rarely appears in practice. You're limited to consulting to clients – and in client processes – that have inherent multi-million dollar savings to be had, or inherent multi-million dollar gains to be had. What if you're a humble accountant who is talented in piecing together company accounts for medium-sized enterprises? Or, what if you're an engineer who specializes in designing road infrastructure? Will these multi-million dollar risk/reward opportunities come by often?

The beauty of creating a successful consulting *enterprise* (which I will define as a firm with people, a structure and a market presence), as distinct from being a successful consultant, is that it can be a phenomenally successful activity. "Million-dollar consulting" becomes an everyday term when you have an enterprise. It requires hard work, but it's not the classical slog of hard work, the type characterized by mind-numbing repetition with incremental career improvement. It's the hard work of working smart. This type of hard work is no less energy-sapping than its classical counterpart, but it does create its own internal energy within you, the consulting entrepreneur, like a perpetual motion machine. And even a small but successful consulting enterprise with you at the helm – the owner/operator – is a powerful vehicle for early financial independence and (if the urge takes you there) an early retirement from the rat race.

Consulting is a bankable industry. But it's a feast-to-famine dynamic. It's hard to find that many mega-consulting firms (compared to other industries) with multi-billion dollar market caps. This makes the industry a slightly unsettling investment prospect in your standard stock exchange. Still, the art of giving advice is alive and well, and it's not likely to die anytime soon. In fact, as the world increases in complexity, the art of advice is likely to thrive. Globalization creates new challenges, which in turn breeds new forms of advice to deal with these challenges. The post-industrial era, the electronic age, post-Global-Financial-Crisis governance, and the increasingly bewildering array of information and misinformation around, makes sound business advice more valuable than ever before. I use the term 'business advice' not to only include 'business management consulting' but to broadly encompass consulting about everything to do with running any kind of commercial or governmental activity, such as engineering, logistics, environmental, economics, human resources, strategy, tactical execution, change management, safety.... the list is very long.

The trouble with advice is: there is a lot of it around. Some of it is unsolicited, and you can find this advice almost anywhere – from mothers-in-law, to passengers on airplanes, to taxi drivers, to almost anyone with an opinion. Of course, not all of it is sound, and most readers might agree that mothers-in-law are a case in point (I apologize for this stereotyping; I've only ever had one of them, but I hear rumors). Some of it is available on the internet, that world-changing platform of informed, uninformed, misinformed and partially informed opinion. Free advice is one of the most available commodities in the world. With a bit of a discerning eye, it's fairly easy to mold old, free advice and re-brand it into new and much more expensive advice. Try it. Ask yourself for advice on something you don't know; for example a strategy to increase productivity in a manufacturing plant, or the conservation of marine vegetation in a dredging operation. With a little bit of direction, you should be able to distil a few hours' of internet research work into a summary advisory document. Ask your above-average high school student; they do some inspired re-hashing of existing knowledge. *What do you call someone who tells you what you already know, then sends you a bill? A consultant.*

In the information age, the barriers to entry for consultants have dropped tremendously. Today – and very likely tomorrow – you don't necessarily have to be an expert at what you do in order to be a paid consultant. You simply need to know more than your client, or have more time to undertake a task than your client does. Access to information is a great leveler in this game. At the same time, the need for consultants has increased, courtesy of the previously mentioned globalization and the deeper connectedness of business decisions with the rest of the world. This has led to a kind of commoditization and de-regulation of consulting, and the increased growth of an industry. But with this boom we also see failed consulting enterprises littering the landscape of advisory services. The sustainable consulting enterprise is a beast that is fast becoming a minority in this industry, while unsustainable consulting two-year-wannabes scurry around the post-GFC landscape with their short half-lives and even shorter attention spans.

There are many excellent books on consulting to be found. The fundamentals of consulting are well known, and the skills and knowledge you need to become a good consultant are at your fingertips. But being a consultant and building a strong consulting firm are two different skill sets. When I started my first consulting firm, I searched exhaustively for resources that would help guide my way. I had so many burning questions that my lists of queries spawned their own sub-lists, like a plague of rabbits with question marks on their quivering fur. Many of the answers were, of course, available in business books and resources. Some of the answers lay in books about consulting. Yet other answers were discovered in books on branding, on innovation, on marketing, on research and even one on manufacturing. In the end, I found out more than I ever wanted to know, and simultaneously failed to find out about some things that I needed to know until I had to grapple with them myself, some years into my first attempt at creating a consulting enterprise.

If you enter consulting to make a quick dollar, or to supplement or bridge your personal income, this book won't offer you much. If, on the other hand, you are hoping to create a sustainable business enterprise that accumulates value – value that you can capitalize on – you should read on.

I started my first consulting firm after roles in government, in industry and in a large and successful consulting organization. The insights I gained in each of my first two roles – in government and in industry – were valuable. They were client organizations; they used consultants. From these I learnt how consultants were chosen. I learnt that choices were made on both objective and subjective information, and a good consulting enterprise was adept at providing both, with a competitive and differentiated edge. The large and successful consulting organization I worked in was a group that had been established in the 1970s and grew, organically and by acquisition, to a global presence with 120 offices. From this I learnt much about the successes and failures of growth models, of brand development, of successful and not-so-successful country entry strategies, and of the two bookends of consulting success – pitch and performance.

When I started my own firm the first time, I had two distinct choices; I could either become a lone consultant or grow a consulting firm. I chose the latter. The consulting fundamentals of both are roughly the same, but the latter organizational challenge is obviously much more consuming. It also brings much more financial and reputational rewards, if done right. Of course I didn't do everything right, and I didn't do everything alone. What I did wrong provided some of my best lessons. What was done right was enough to grow my first firm in five years so that it had operations in Europe, South Africa, Asia and Australia with multinational clients and very high client retention. This last characteristic – the high client retention – added tremendous value to the organization, and was one of the key reasons that the value of the firm grew very strongly. For that first attempt, it took five years to grow a highly profitable company that carried no debt. It had loyal staff, high profits, and a high capital value that was still growing when I sold that first enterprise.

During the journey, and subsequent journeys, I learned a great deal; some through lessons from others, and some through my own trial-and-error attempts. Many of my strategies worked well, others needed tinkering before they worked, and others proved to be poor strategies. I learned from others by asking questions and thinking through their answers carefully. And you often learn more from your mistakes than you do from your successes. Never underestimate the value of failed experiments.

### The reluctant consultant

*One of my colleagues is a university professor who, once upon a time, was a respected consultant in finance and economics. He ran his own firm for a few years, sold it and went into academia. I asked Colin if he ever regretted not maintaining his consulting practice and skills. Did he 'settle' too early?*

*"I was never consulting material," he told me. I was astonished. From what I knew of Colin, and what I had seen, I'd always thought of*

*him as the quintessential consultant. A problem-solver extraordinaire, his career was peppered with country-scale consulting to the World Bank, the International Finance Corporation and others.*

*"I can see you need an explanation," he observed, grinning. "I found consulting to be – frankly –seedy."*

*I gasped. Then looked offended. He continued, insensitively,*

*"Quality gets compromised for the billable hour. It's cut-throat, you compete on price half the time. Which impacts on quality. You profess to know the answer when in fact you only have a sense of how to get the answer. It just felt like smoke and mirrors. After a while, it wasn't for me."*

*I protested. Colin's work had been groundbreaking, and was still being referred to almost fifteen years later when devising country economic policies. Surely he's disproved his point right there?*

*"I found the majority of consulting to be the low level junk, price competitive and value-compromised," he said. "Once in a while we'd get assignments that were unique, and we built our reputation on them, but most of what we did was mundane." He paused, and then made what I thought was his most important point. "But maybe that was because we didn't get our niche right."*

## The three forms of consulting

Consulting, at its core, is the application of an informed opinion. You're handing out advice. What makes your advice valuable in creating value for the client is (1) how knowledgeably informed you are, and (2) how insightful your opinion is. This is important, because if you only do two things right, these are the two things to get right.

Being knowledgeably informed does not mean you are a walking encyclopedia (and although that never hurts, not many people can genuinely claim that they are). The most valuable piece of consulting is called for when there is a problem, and the solution is not evident. There's no existing knowledge that cuts-and-pastes to fix the problem. Big problem plus no solution equals wringing hands, wailing and gnashing of teeth. Consternation. If there is a problem and you need a solution, your big gun is *analysis*. You're trying to figure out why the problem exists, or why the problem might in the future exist, and then you're trying to work out how to make it cease to exist. So the 'informed' part of your informed opinion hinges on analysis.

Your informed opinion is not as bland as the average point of view. Everyone has a point of view, and people are unlikely to pay much for a point of view. That is, unless there is something special about it; something extra, perhaps like the depth of analysis you bring. They may not even listen to your opinion, for free, at parties, unless you have this something extra.

But there is more. Your valuable opinion is framed through analysis, but it is brought to life with *insight*. Insight is the difference between a problem solved theoretically, and a problem solved effectively and efficiently.

Your armory comprises analysis and insight, and if you have these then your consulting enterprise is off to a very good start. If your armory comprises knowledge and opinion, you still have a decent shot at consulting, but it may not be terribly different from your competitors.

All of which brings us to what I believe are the three basic forms of consulting.

*Growing and Selling a Successful Consulting Firm*

## Bodyshopping

Each form of consulting activity has a different value to a client. The first form is what I call *bodyshopping*. In bodyshopping, the client hires a consultant to do a task that he or she cannot do because of time or resource pressures. The client (either the individual or the organization) is quite capable of undertaking the task, but for one reason or another, it's not near the top of their personal to-do list. A client resorts to bodyshopping when deadlines are tight, or there aren't enough people to undertake the task in the time available, or the task is commoditized in some way (for example the tasks are a 'lower level' task for your organization) or human resource (for example 'headcount') constraints force you to outsource a task. If I hire a gardener to prune my hedges, something I could probably do if I was so inclined and had the time, I have just made a bodyshopping transaction. As you would imagine, bodyshopping is generally not top-dollar consulting, unless time pressures are extreme and the task is critical.

Globalization did interesting things to the bodyshopping proposition. It made it more attractive. It made it much easier to access, from outside of a client organization, lower-value and non-core skills. As a result of easier access, the available pool of bodyshopping resources expanded dramatically. Witness the birth, rise and continued rise of outsourced services such as call centers and IT service providers. The activity morphed from a consulting proposition to a large scale contracting proposition. The consulting propositions I discuss in this book are not of this extreme variety; I will confine my comments to more modest and much smaller-scale bodyshopping concepts.

### The carpenter who became a consultant

*One of my favorite success stories is of an old University pal, David. David had worked for a while, in the building industry as a carpenter, before deciding on formal education, in this case engineering. When he joined the University, he was quite a bit older than his peers. He had a cool car (compared to students like me, who drove clapped-out third-hand junk heaps), a steady girlfriend and a modest apartment; three attributes that made him the envy of many. During the longer semester breaks, he would hire a bunch of contractors and build a house for a client. He did it quickly and efficiently, and took care of all the pesky details and project management that his clients wanted to avoid.*

*By the time David graduated, he was completely disinterested in finding a job. While the rest of us competed ferociously in the job market, David got himself a loan and continued his building enterprise. He hired people like himself who would build houses – they could hire the right tradespeople, manage the procurement and delivery of materials; all of the menial details that clients preferred not to concern themselves with. He expanded, from housing, to local Council developments, to roads, rail and infrastructure.*

*He never looked back, building a strong firm whose base of income was derived from bodyshopping. In other words, doing what the client could not be bothered doing, and hiring lots of people to get the work done. He only made a small percentage profit on each person he hired, but he hired a lot of people. And so, like the millionaire who became rich by selling one-dollar widgets, he created success from the bulk selling of people-hours who offered nothing special or unique, but filled a void in the market that asked for a high volume of this commodity.*

## Knowledge-based consulting

The second form of consulting can be thought of as *knowledge-based* consulting. This form of consulting accesses unique knowledge or skills that the consultant may possess. This is a rarer commodity in the market for the client to access. Consequently, the client may not have the skills in-house (and may never want to, especially if the knowledge or skill is only applied sporadically). This form of consulting commands a premium. This premium increases with the rarity of the knowledge or skill being applied, and the value it unleashes for the client.

The beauty of knowledge-based consulting is that it seems to be a perpetual-motion machine. The more complex our world gets, the more the world of niche, knowledge-based consulting expands. And the more niche, knowledge-based activities are propagated, the more complex our world gets.

A new gas economy sees us creating lower-carbon fuels and exporting them into markets to feed growing energy demands and an increasing reluctance to exploit higher-carbon fossil fuels. In this evolving fuel economy, knowledge-based innovations make the fuel transfer proposition more efficient, more productive and more adaptive to growing energy economies. This in turn helps propagate a more vibrant and diverse gas economy, which creates more need for innovative efficiencies and differentiators, and so on. See? Complexity never dies. Knowledge-based consultants have a bright future.

Continuing with the metaphor of the gardener, an example of knowledge-based consulting might be picking the trees and shrubs, the potting mixes and irrigation systems that are best suited to the climate and soils around my house. The key purchase is knowledge.

### The sibling consultants

*I used to think people who went back to university to get their PhDs were nerds who could think of nothing better to do. Worse, when I was a young engineer, I used to think that people who 'specialized' were painting themselves into some kind of corner. I had this kind of reverse snobbishness when it came to professional skills; common was good, rare was snooty and unwanted. Over time, I realized this was a naïve view. Specialized knowledge is rare, and like all rare commodities, it commands a hefty price. Of course, demand for rare commodities may not be as high as other commodities. So you have a hefty price but low volume.*

*Chris and Kelly were a brother-and-sister team in the year above mine who, with their twin First-Class-Honors degrees, landed scholarships to do their PhDs. In a stroke of genius – which in my mind justified their First Class Honors results more convincingly than their academic colors – they did PhDs in related areas. This effectively meant that they harnessed not one, but two knowledge-based disciplines, and joined them together. Four years later, they opened up a niche consulting arm – an arcane area of high strength steel in bridges and virtuoso architectural buildings – in their father's consulting firm. There was virtually no competition, at least in a 2000-mile radius.*

*Their challenge, which is not uncommon in knowledge-based consulting, is that they were short of understudies to capitalize on this niche market. In other words, growth in that niche market was hampered by the lack of people with their rarified knowledge. And they had no significant mentoring program to speak of, to create clones of themselves. So while they commanded high consulting fees for themselves, there was limited leverage. Now, some people strive for this rarified knowledge base partly because there is no competition. However, it is a double-edged sword. The consulting proposition can start, and end, with you – leaving you without many growth prospects and a limited exit strategy.*

## Value-based consulting

The third form of consulting is what I called *value-based* consulting. In value-based consulting, insight and problem-solving acumen is applied to a situation. The value of value-based consulting depends on the organizational value that the solved problem brings to the client organization. If it sounds circular, that's because it is. If a client organization wants to, say, transform its supply chain efficiency, and the savings the transformation brings is $1m per year for many years to come, the consultancy is worth around $2m (if you believe, as many would, that a two-year return on investment is attractive).

Value-based consulting is less expansive than the other two; I've observed that it occupies a relatively small space in the consulting world. You might assume that knowledge-based consulting would be the smaller niche because specialist knowledge is rare. But the logic says otherwise. Value-based consulting is applied to more unique problems. After all, if the same problem had been solved a few times before, the ability to solve the problem again has probably become a knowledge-based consultancy proposition. Value-based consulting requires thought leadership and innovation, and innovation by definition is a bit of a one-off proposition.

The gardener I hired in this example might be expected to design the garden around my house so that it has the appropriate feng shui, the mix of landscape elements that imparts a certain character that I favor, synergy with the design of the house and the potential to add considerably to the resale value of the property. For another property, which might have different slopes and soils and a completely different architectural layout to the building, there is a different unique value proposition.

### The lazy consultant

*Most consulting firms claim to 'add value' and most claim innovative abilities. This is because, in the world of consulting, value-based outcomes are prized. For the consultant, it has considerable reputational value and, among consultants, it is a class differentiator. First class consulting has value-based outcomes, second-class consulting is something anyone can do. Many consultants aspire to the value-based brand.*

*The client rewards you not for the hours worked, but for the outcome produced (although you'll still be expected to account for the hours worked!) But what hourly rate do you place on genius? Does it matter if it only took me three days to produce a masterpiece of consulting that will transform your organization and net you a million dollars? Would you pay fifty thousand dollars for that piece of genius, or in excess of fifteen thousand dollars a day for that demonstrable value? I would.*

*An early consulting mentor with an off-beat sense of humor once gave me an invaluable piece of advice. On a long flight and three wines into the meal service I was (dangerously, given that he was my boss' boss), confessing that my vision was not to work for a consulting firm, but to run my own firm. He said, "Let me give you some advice then. For every five hard-working consultants you hire, make sure you have at least one who's inherently lazy. Lazy, but not afraid of hard work, that's important, you understand? That kind of consultant is always, ALWAYS, searching for an easier way to do their job, an easier way to do everything. When they find value, they REALLY find value."*

*I was enthralled.*

*"But don't let that be YOU on this assignment," he finished, dryly.*

## Your shelf life

So, on the sliding scale of consultancy value, bodyshopping is worth less (per unit of effort) than knowledge-based consulting, which in turn is worth less (per unit of effort) than value-based consulting. Obviously this is not a hard-and-fast rule; for example, a bodyshopping assignment on a critical deadline might be worth more to a client than a more leisurely knowledge-based assignment. And of course, consulting assignments can be hybrids of two or more of the three forms of consultancy outlined.

Why is your understanding of the forms of consultancy important in creating your own enterprise? Other than the obvious (they help define the 'chargeout rate' or revenue base of a consultancy), they also impact heavily on how you shape your offering in the market, how you recruit into your firm, and how you remunerate and reward your staff.

But much of consulting has a short shelf-life. The higher-value end of consulting is, much like a bright star that burns out quickly, often of fleeting value. This is because we live in an age of information, where knowledge continues to expand at an astonishing rate and the increasing complexity of the world requires greater insights to be successful. This is not a bad thing, because it means high-value consulting regenerates itself through knowledge and innovation. The solution that worked yesterday may work less well today, and less well again tomorrow. And this means more work, more analysis and insight is re-quired to deliver value. But it also means the competitive edge is fierce, and staying on top of your game is essential. At the lower-value end of consulting, the pace is less frenetic and the pressure to analysis and regenerate insights is much less.

Consultants are like gunslingers for hire. If you have a problem, you bring one in. You don't want them around for long, because they are expensive. And they are not of your kind. They don't belong in your firm. Their culture is not yours. Just like the gunslinger who doesn't belong in your town, you want to see them gone when the job is done. In Japan, they are *ronin*, masterless samurai, people of ambiguous loy-alties. They are, to be sure, potent and talented, but there is a vague tragedy about their existence just outside the hub of society.

And despite its glamour, the consultant's life can be profession-ally unfulfilling. Clients can ask for advice, and they will pay for it, but they don't have to take your advice. A good consultant finds solu-tions to problems, and some of those solutions are not that popular. If you recommend a client downsizes, or strengthens management to make better decisions, or spends millions of dollars in retrofitting their operation, these are all painful actions. As most gunslingers probably know, the adage is true: you can take a horse to water, but you can't make it drink. As a consultant, you spend a lot of time seeing what *could be*, and then watching – unfulfilled – as it never *is*. Sometimes your advice is taken, and sometimes it is not. You learn to move on, never owning the problem or the solution. If you're passionate about your work, which is an asset to any consultant, there can often be a sense of emptiness about some of your work, a sense of futility. Older consultants, like their grizzled gunslinger counterparts, can be deeply cynical. They are too easily able to see faults and too easily able to shrug and walk away without guilt if their advice is not taken. They are too ready to see good intentions undone by inadequate commitment.

Like everything in life, consulting has its own yin and yang. But at its heart, it is a dynamic and lucrative world. It is slightly mysterious, the phrase *I am a consultant* managing to span the breadth of ambiguity between trusted advisor and assassin-for-hire. And its beauty is that anyone who knows something can be a consultant. The barriers to entry into the consulting world are astoundingly low.

## THREE TIPS

*Tip one*: Remember, there are essentially three types of consulting. Be very clear about what type of consulting you want to offer, and – if you choose a hybrid – how much of each component of the hybrid you have. The lower down the value chain, the less challenging it is to execute…but it also means that the pace of activity required to achieve higher profits might be more frenetic. Be crystal clear about your choice.

*Tip two*: Make sure you are genuinely cut out – personally, emotionally, professionally – for consulting. Think of the analogy to *ronin* that was made earlier – those masterless samurai. Is that you? No-one else can tell you whether you are or not.

*Tip three*: Be good (top-percentile good) at something in your field. When you first start, your personal credibility is everything. Clients and employees alike will be drawn to unique and valued skill sets. What are yours?

# CHAPTER 2
# THE EXIT STRATEGY

*If you want a happy ending, that depends, of course,*
*on where you stop your story.*
*– Orson Welles*

## Writing your story backwards

My philosophy has always been to start with the exit strategy, which some people find startling. There is a dispassionate cold-bloodedness to this approach, I'm told. Passionate professionals who love their work might feel like this is too calculating, almost heresy. *What about the people you hire? Aren't you starting with an abandonment mindset? Shouldn't you wait and see how it goes before forming an exit strategy?* Others warm to my philosophy, because it brings a finite purpose to the enterprise. Nothing focuses the mind as much as a finite purpose, an end for which the means must be created.

I assert that it's not as odd as it seems to start an enterprise with an exit strategy, and particularly consulting enterprises. Consulting enterprises are not like retail chains or telecommunications or mining companies. Their worth lies very much in their people, and the solutions they create and execute. When starting a consulting enterprise, that worth is you, the key person. At some point you're going to want to retire, and you might not necessarily want the worth of your enterprise to go to pasture with you. Of course, it is a viable option, but it may not be the best option for you.

Some readers might want to grow a consulting enterprise and sell a successful, thriving business to a buyer. Cashing out and moving onto something else is an elegant way to create a step-improvement in financial independence, and create options for your life path. Others might want to grow a consulting enterprise to see them through a successful career and then a part-time retirement. Whatever your motivation, you need to spend some time on it and clearly define it to yourself. This vision is the backdrop, the horizon and the driver for the blueprint of your strategy.

It is much easier to nurse your consulting enterprise into your retirement than to plan to sell it. It's not so much an exit strategy as a moving-in strategy, and there is no significant gear change to plan for. You set your cruise control until you run out of fuel. Although many of the insights in this book work well enough for a moving-in strategy, there is a sense of urgency that you will pick up while reading the next few chapters. That sense of urgency assumes you have a defined-target exit strategy; perhaps the creation of a high-value enterprise that you can leave, in exchange for some capital, in a reasonably short period of time.

If you want to exit at some point – cash out – you need a very well defined strategy. The more you are inclined to 'see how it goes', the tougher it will be to execute an exit strategy. Clarity is incredibly important here.

While it's certainly important, the reality is that some of your valiant striving for clarity might not actually result in one-hundred-percent clarity. That's OK. The key thing is that you search relentlessly for clarity, and know that every morsel you pick up will add up to a greater degree of clarity. Until, suddenly, your exit strategy starts to crystallize into something that you don't just hope for, but you actually believe in. It's a bit like visualizing a high jump, running over and over in your mind the small details that, together, result in a successful clearing of the bar. With enough visualization and attention to clarity and detail, your mind moves from "I think I can" to "I know I will".

### Comfort with ambiguity

*These days, in a corporation, many leadership programs are built around the concept of comfort with ambiguity. Great value is placed on being able to set clear direction with a clear 'why' even if the data you have is fuzzy, the future is in flux and all of the moving parts of your decision points are rotating at once.*

*A CEO of a multinational company whom I spent quite a lot of time with, during an extended transformation assignment that lasted some years, remarked that he had met many consultants who, surprisingly to him, abhorred ambiguity.*

*"Yet you'd think that your line of work is all about ambiguity. How long does your cashflow projection last? Three months? Mine lasts several years. Your contracts are a few months on average. Mine are five to ten year supply contracts. Consulting careers are inherently ambiguous. So why then are many consultants so uncomfortable with ambiguity?"*

*I asked him what made him think that.*

*"My experience is that far too many consultants cut-and-paste solutions from one problem to another. Maybe that's one way to achieve efficiency, but I wonder if they have taken on the project BECAUSE they already have a cut-and-paste solution in mind. Consultants will willingly work on an hourly rate for no fixed scope, but are wary of starting fixed-price contracts unless the problem and outcome are clear. And when I suggest a risk-reward contract, they almost run out the door in panic!"*

*It's a paradox, but I think he had a point. Consulting organizations are populated by individuals who are fine with proposing a hypothesis for their clients, because they don't have to live with the outcome themselves. Are there many consultants who take risk/reward contracts? These are contracts where, for example, you work for a minimum retainer but if your solution works, you get paid a proportion of the upside. So, low pay with the potential of very high pay if you do the job well? The answer is no.*

*And that is indeed a telling point about the mettle of the average consultant.*

## Know your financial perspectives

If you are going to cash out on your exit strategy, you need to understand the transaction from two perspectives. Yours, as the seller, is obviously one perspective. The other is your buyer. It is important to understand how a consulting enterprise might be valued by a buyer. To be honest, the buyer's perspective is probably more important than yours.

Let's consider the two angles. First, there is a simple equation that determines a possible sale value:

*Enterprise value =*
*(Multiplier x average net profit) + Assets – Liabilities*

It's very important to understand this equation, because key decisions around your exit strategy pivot around what it tells you. Let's break it down, leaving the multiplier to the end.

The average net profit is what your buyer might hope to gain every year as a result of buying your enterprise. If the buyer does nothing to your enterprise but continues to manage it as you have, he or she is entitled to expect that the average profit would stay much the same, all other things being equal.

The average net profit can be calculated a variety of ways, but using the average of the last three years' profit before sale is a reasonable benchmark, if the profit has been relatively stable or has grown somewhat from year to year.

Assets are the tangible things that the company holds (cash in the bank, equipment and debtors, for example). For a consulting company, unless you have a lot of cash in the bank, or you own the office premises, or you have high-capital value equipment, this may not be a significant factor.

Liabilities are the opposite of assets (like loans and creditors). Consulting companies can run up significant loans or creditors, and for poorly managed enterprises this can be a significant factor that devalues the firm.

The multiplier is the wildcard in your equation. It is a composite of several characteristics of your enterprise; its goodwill with clients, the stability of its workforce, the portfolio of clients, how long it's been operating successfully, and so on. It's a measure of reliability of the money-making machine.

Every accountant you speak to will have a different view of what the multiplier should be. (Then again, every accountant you speak to has a different view on everything financial, so don't be surprised if you get multiple answers to your multiplier question). A good consulting enterprise (displaying strong goodwill, a stable workforce, a diverse portfolio of clients across economic sectors and a long history) might command a multiplier of between 2 and 3 (and sometimes more, in the right economic climate). It will command a lot less if you're a one-person consulting show because the enterprise is too heavily reliant on you. You become what's known as a "key-person risk".

If you have a cash-out figure in mind, it is then reasonably straightforward (using the formula) to work out the average of three years' profit that would need to be generated to get you close to that cash-out figure. It doesn't have to be exact, but you will want to have quite a good sense of what it is.

The second simple equation is your internal rate of return, which financial professionals call the IRR. The IRR represents what the buyer might be able to do with the enterprise once he or she buys it, and how this translates into a return on capital invested. The IRR is a discounted cash flow calculation; in other words it considers, on the basis of a repeating income over some time, how much should be paid in capital at the start to 'buy' that income.

It is worth understanding the IRR of the transaction because it gives you an insight into the *relative* worth of your company compared to other options the buyer might have (such as starting their own firm, or acquiring a different firm, or investing in something else entirely). The calculation of an internal rate of return is well documented in many financial textbooks, so I will not repeat it here. For large infrastructure that might operate for dozens of years, an IRR of 11% to 14% might be considered reasonable. For smaller, shorter-lived investments, a higher IRR might be more suitable.

If the buyer plans to do nothing with the enterprise and/or your annual profit is constant, then the IRR calculation might give you only slightly more insight than the enterprise value equation. But if the buyer might do something more than mine the profits of your enterprise – for example, leverage growth or facilitate an entry strategy into a new market for him or her – then it is worth considering the IRR. Also, if the buyer purchases your enterprise while it is still increasing its net profits (or, alternatively, decreasing) then the IRR calculation is quite useful to understand your potential negotiating stance. The IRR calculation is another useful data point which helps clarify when in the life of your enterprise you can maximize your exit strategy outcomes.

When you work out your exit strategy, start with these figures. You will select a figure that is informed by these calculations. This may be your retirement fund, or your fund to invest in other things, or simply a measure of the profit you want to make after some years of investment in your enterprise. Now, if this sounds like a not-very-inspirational way to start defining your exit strategy, don't despair. All you're doing at this stage is deciding what you want out of your entre-preneurial effort.

## The challenge of an exit strategy

Exiting a business is not as easy as exiting a café after you're done with your chocolate croissant and macchiato. There is a very impor-tant rule in exit strategies, and it is this: you have to be *allowed* to exit. If a larger company – let's call them Heavy Hitters Inc. – buys out your enterprise, they will look at where the money is coming from within your company. If the revenue is largely attributed to you, there are two ways the deal could go.

One way is that they value your enterprise a whole lot less than it's really worth, because an important part of the machinery (you) is hell-bent on retiring to Bermuda. Or you've been eating too many croissants and you're going to check out some other way. The point is, there is a bit of a risk that you're not going to be there tomorrow, and you're a bit too important for the buyer to ignore that.

Assuming that your health and longevity is not too much in question, another approach is that the deal comes resplendent with bling, in the form of a 'golden handcuff'. The golden handcuff might include a clause that says they will pay you for the company over three years (or some other period that interferes with your flight bookings to Bermuda), with the payment related to the profit that the company makes over those years. If your profit slides, so does the payment. And Mr, Ms or Mrs Heavy Hitter will make sure the penalty for sliding profits is high when your wrists are adorned with the 'cuffs. Tight golden handcuffs won't pay you a simple third of the value every year; they will pay you, for example, 20% in year one, 35% in year two and 45% in year three. In other words, most of your payout will occur towards the end of the term. It can be quite frustrating. There is a reason they are called golden handcuffs. You are a prisoner.

If you're happy with this – and many are – then good for you. One of my colleagues said she thought of it as parole, not so much as incarceration. She had a fair point, and she did exit her enterprise elegantly. But I urge you to think more creatively.

See, it's one thing to be *allowed* to exit, and it's another (much better) thing to be *encouraged* to exit. There is a lower likelihood of golden handcuffs being slapped on your wrists. So how do you set your strategy so that you will be encouraged to exit? Turning up to work without your pants will not do the trick; at least not in the way you expect it to. What is more likely to work is being a dead weight on the enterprise, a near-useless add-on who, unfortunately for Mr, Ms or Mrs Heavy Hitter, owns a lot of shares.

The buyer will look at where the money is coming from, and if you're not in that part of the scenery, you're more likely to be encouraged to exit. This encouragement will occur quicker if you're drawing a handsome salary and holding too many shares for your own good. It will be done with smiles and pomp and fanfare, it will be done more quickly, and you'll be on your way to Bermuda with a warm feeling of goodwill, the buzz of good champagne and a healthier bank balance. An elegant exit.

Forming an exit strategy in which you're the first redundancy is a sublime way to maximize your returns. But it's not easy. On day one, you're the rainmaker, the daily grind machine, the accountant, the photocopier, the report binder and the mailperson. On the day you exit, you want to be only slightly more useful than garden furniture in a 38th floor double-glazed office. How do you make that happen? Can you do it, or will your pride intervene? We'll come to that, but note for now that how you choose to make yourself less and less useful, is an essential part of your exit strategy.

There's another important rule in forming exit strategies. Don't be in debt. If your enterprise is in debt, getting out can be slow and laborious. After the Global Financial Crisis in the late 2000s, the not-so-affectionately-termed GFC, any semblance of tolerance for debt went out the window. Carrying debt brought deep suspicion and a lot of due diligence from buyers. Financiers suddenly wanted to check every minute detail of the debtor, down to DNA-level due diligence, before accepting debt-laden assets and enterprises. Debt went from being a load you could shoulder – in fact, once upon a time it made you look positively heroic and accountants applauded a well-geared balance sheet for its efficiency – to being the equivalent of deal-busting quicksand.

Yet another, fairly obvious, rule in exit strategies is to avoid exiting in a down market, and to time your exit on an upward trajectory. Buyers pay quickly and well (and there are more of them to fight over your enterprise) when there is some way to go before you arrive at the peak of growth and profit performance, and if it's evident you're on the right bearing to get there. There's a bit less you can do about this one, as market forces can be fickle and you may not be blessed with the psychic ability to foresee the ups and downs.

It's important to understand not just your business, but the business of your clients and the market forces that affect them. In other words, be an economist of sorts. In the absence of psychic powers, one way to reduce the risk of market forces upsetting your plans is to think about your client portfolio and apply basic economic logic to it.

Create a safer environment for yourself by ensuring you have a balanced portfolio. If one client sector goes down, your business shouldn't go down with it, or suffer unreasonably because of it.

### Start with a vision

*Before I started my first enterprise I was working for a large consulting firm; one with 110 offices globally; one that had started in the*

*1970s with two entrepreneurs and had grown over the decades to a firm with an A-list brand. I knew one of the founding entrepreneurs and had met the other on occasions. Stories about them were legendary and, once I actually met them, I found the stories quite plausible. They were impressive, visionary gentlemen. I had spent some time speaking with one of these men and had distilled, over two or three years, some gems of wisdom. These gems crystallized over time in my mind and, refined by my own thoughts and ideas, began to form a basic strategy.*

*One day, two colleagues, each with their own successful one-person consulting practice, took me out for dinner. They suggested I should do what they had done; hang out my shingle and join their band of one-man bands. We could form an alliance of sorts, they said. Provide each other with overflow work when one or the other was swamped. Synergy.*

*The red wine flowed freely and, having known each other for many years, the conversation was irreverent and funny. We formed a noisy table, overlooking a river on which ferry lights danced and the pinpoint-lighted silhouettes of bridges framed the evening sky.*

*Halfway through our third bottle of wine, deep into our second course, I declined their suggestion. I was in my mid-30s, with energy to burn, I said. Seven years on, I wanted to be able to retire if I wanted. A one-person practice wasn't going to do that for me. A thirty or forty person practice might though. A hundred-person practice probably would.*

*I caught sardonic grins. What, in seven years?*

*Yep, I said. Set it up to sell from year one. And I think it can be done pretty easily, without much capital. I asked the waiter for his pen and some large sheets of paper, and explained my decision with an exit strategy. If you focus on the exit strategy, your mindset changes. Rather than simply focusing on a successful business, you focus on the build, and rate of build; and the stabilization and rate of stabilization. It makes you think differently, and I'd spent a couple of years thinking differently.*

*I scribbled some numbers, drew some graphs and somewhere in the process I sketched Spiderman. In hindsight I'm not sure what Spiderman had to do with my Exit Strategy. Perhaps I was suggesting that we could each be superheroes of our own destinies. (Did I mention the three bottles of wine?).*

*Less than eight years later, we'd each done exactly that. We'd each built enterprises of strength and value. It turns out it wasn't that hard.*

## Predicting the unpredictable

One important feature of your Exit Strategy is that it must be flexible. Not so flexible that it disappears altogether when times change, of course. But the reality is that you may grow your enterprise faster than you thought. Or slower. Your succession planning may go well, or poorly. The point here is that seven or ten or fifteen years is a long time, and you should start by being supremely confident that at least some of your assumptions will turn out to be inaccurate.

Inaccuracy is not something to be feared. It's a fact of life, so anticipate it. In the world of process engineering in the 1980s, lots of process failure analyses were created and evolved. They had names like Fault Tree Analysis, and Failure Mode and Event Analysis. They were designed to systematically analyze where things could go wrong. But my favorite analysis was the much less scientifically termed What-If Analysis. Anyone could do this analysis, although its low entry threshold did mean that some fairly ridiculous What-If questions were asked. The operating rule for this analysis was "there are no stupid questions", mostly to alleviate the fear that might constrain people from asking questions that others might laugh at.

My tip is, use the What-If analysis on your Exit Strategy. Question all the things you believe to be facts in your Exit Strategy, and then ask some sillier questions. You'll be amazed at how well you test your Exit Strategy. What if some enterprises had asked, "What if there's a Global Financial Crisis"? Many companies that folded during that dark economic period might have stood a better chance of surviving. Ask your family, friends, significant other and any other trusted confidantes to help you wreck your Exit Strategy. You'll be too close to the strategy to see some things, and you'll be defensive. They will ask questions that sit in your blind spot. They will also ask silly questions, so be prepared for that. Good humor helps. You'll probably go back to the drawing board once or twice to finesse your Exit Strategy, because unless you're a Grand Master of chess or a Zen strategist, your first attempt will have flaws that can be exposed. But it will benefit from this testing.

Let's start with the cash out figure. This is going to be iterative, because as you get into the exercise and you build your plan, you'll change it. You may find that you become very confident that you can achieve the first number, and you might revise it upwards. Or you might find that it takes too long to achieve the first number, and you revise it downwards. Everyone's number will be different. Be reasonably specific. If you simply want to be a millionaire, that's too vague. How many millions of dollars? 1.5 million? 4.0 million? 7.3 million? 17 million? It's useful to think about what you want to do with the money, and then work backwards. What do you want to do when you exit? Put the kids through university? Pay off your mortgages and buy other property? Invest in startup companies? Spend a lot of time on a beach? Live off the interest of the remainder? Start a new career path?

Become a perennially unpaid artist or writer? Some of the above? All of the above?

It's part daydreaming and part analysis, but it gives you the first data point in your vision. You should have a number. Without it, you don't have an anchor for your analysis.

From this number, you'll work out the average profit your enterprise has to make three years running (at least) for you to be reasonably confident that you can hit that number. You'll have a lower and upper bound by now, because the goodwill multiplier might be at the lower or upper end of the scale. You might overlay this with your IRR analysis, if you have a very good idea of what a buyer might want to do with the enterprise you create.

Now you'll want to figure out how you become redundant in this enterprise over that period of time, unless of course you accept that a golden handcuff is part of your Exit Strategy.

Becoming redundant is a very tricky proposition, particularly if you also want to be able to positively and compellingly influence the realization of your Exit Strategy at the time of your exit. You need to have enough management control, and enough shareholder voting rights, to steer the outcome in the direction you need. But at the same time, in order to become redundant, you have to give away some (and probably a sizeable portion) of management control to others in your staff. So this means that by the time you are ready to execute your Exit Strategy, you'll want to have people who do what you do (and perhaps they do what you do even better than you do it yourself).

Although it's theoretically possible to hold 100% of the shares at the time of your Exit Strategy, it's not a practical expectation to have. Your people should have skin in the game – a reason to stay and make the Exit Strategy work – during the potentially tumultuous period of sale and your exit. If your key people don't have equity in the outcome of the sale, there is a greater likelihood that your enterprise will crumble. Key people might leave. So an important part of your thinking has to be the shape of the equity holdings at your time of exit, which is related to your potential structure at the time of exit. And this, in turn, is related to your consulting model, the number of offices you have, and the practices you run within your enterprise. Of course, you're not a psychic so you don't know these with any kind of confidence. So you make assumptions. Now, hopefully, you can see why the calculations are iterative. There are a few parameters to think through, and you can virtually guarantee that all of them will vary from your base assumptions.

If you have less than 100% of the shares, then it stands to reason that the real dollar amount you get from selling is less than the figure you started estimating with. This is one of the reasons your planning will be highly iterative. Be prepared to map scenario after scenario, and commit to patient and careful consideration of your analysis. Go back to the Exit number and alter it – over and over – until you get what you want, with the distributed shareholdings.

Quite some time later, you've run quite a few spreadsheets. You've got variables on multipliers and variables on shareholding arrangements. You've got at least one, and perhaps several, thumbnail sketches of the corporate structure at exit. You've got What-if scenarios. After a while, you've got a sense of how robust your plan is.

Scientists have a way of making sense out of lots of What-If scenarios. They have a method of analysis called the Monte Carlo analysis, which runs variable after variable, and change after change of assumptions, until a set of likely outcomes becomes evident. Monte

Carlo analyses run millions of such scenarios. Obviously you won't have time to run millions of analyses, but you should try to assess as many scenarios as you can, until you become confident that you can see a set of likely outcomes, and you are comfortable with these potential outcomes.

## Creating flexibility

You might quite sensibly ask at this point if it's possible to do all this without knowing *exactly* what type of consulting you (the enterprise) are going to be doing at the point of exit. Yes it is, because these analyses will cause you to think about the core consulting competencies you'll need to create to get to this Exit Strategy. Of course, you'll need to know *generally* what type of consulting organization you're considering (value-based, knowledge-based, bodyshopping or a hybrid), but at this point you don't need precise detail. We're still creating an Exit Strategy, not a Business Plan.

The debilitating trap here is to think at this point that you can't achieve the Exit Strategy number you'd like to, and revise your thinking downwards. If you had a healthy Exit Strategy number, you'll have what looks like a daunting enterprise to create. But if you think small you'll achieve small, so keep thinking as big as you need. Spend more time and determination working out how you can achieve your preferred Exit Strategy outcome, rather than altering your Exit Strategy to suit your conservatism.

Endurance athletes focus on one step at a time. If they contemplated the hill above them during the race, they would feel slightly dismayed. In that dismayed mindset, in order to overcome the hill, they would need to increase their mental strength and wattage considerably. They will run a much more effective race if they are not burdened with a dismayed feeling during the event; if they concentrate on their one-step-at-a-time focus.

Before the race, however, endurance athletes contemplate the hills and they visualize how to get over them. They don't ruefully accept a pessimistic outlook and seek smaller hills or a different race to participate in.

It's worth mentioning the possibility that your Exit Strategy can also take the form of selling out to your staff. It's possible, but it is a slightly longer shot than selling out to Heavy Hitters Inc. If you build a capital asset worth a significant amount of money, then it is possible that for many salaried people – your people – the price of a decent shareholding in such a company might be similar to a mortgage. And given that many of your staff might already be shouldering the burden of a mortgage, you may not find many buyers. You could certainly find shareholders, but it is less likely you'll find a consortium of employee-buyers.

To overcome this, you could sell slowly. Selling down a little bit every year can make the proposition more attractive to your staff, but this is not much different to a golden handcuff. In addition, this introduces internal politics to your Exit Strategy, which is never a good thing. Perhaps several staff members hope to be Managing Director when you leave. Incremental equity sales to staff with the intention of allowing you to exit, creates plenty of room for maneuvering in the ranks of your employees. The time taken to think of these maneuvers detracts from the time taken to make the business a profitable entity. Your first priority should be to maintain a high and consistent profitability, and a strong growth trajectory. This requires client focus by your staff, not a focus on internal shareholding and jostling for position.

Overall, and despite its validity as an option, this option comes with several significant challenges that affect the execution of your Exit Strategy.

If you are looking to sell your company to a bigger firm, then part of forming your Exit Strategy (before you start your company) is to look at who's buying what in your market, and why. There has, in my experience over twenty-five years, including on either side of the Global Financial Crisis, been considerable acquisition activity in the consulting market. In other words, there is a lot of information to be gathered, and much of it has a local or national flavor, as well as differences depending on whether the consulting is in the legal, engineering, financial or other sectors. The intelligence gathering takes time, so be prepared to invest in research. It is likely that you will find different scales of transactions. For example, you might find that the number of consultancies of around twenty staff that are acquired is very high, and that there were fewer acquisitions of companies with staff of a hundred or more. You might find that mergers, rather than acquisitions, occur in the larger companies. This type of intelligence helps you understand what buyer targets you might need to consider in executing your Exit Strategy.

It is worth doing a case study on an acquisition. This is best done from a seller's perspective. Spending time with principals who have sold their companies is a very enlightening experience. Understanding what they would have done similarly or differently if they could wind back the clock is a very useful exercise for you to undertake.

If you speak to enough of them, you'll absorb a diversity of opinion, and you'll see common themes. One of the very important common-theme lessons I learnt was about preserving the company culture. If you have spent time and energy building a successful consulting firm, the last thing you need is for the sale process to fray its successful culture. Selling a company can be debilitating for staff, particularly if you have built the company from scratch. Like it or not, you become the patriarch or the matriarch, and leaving your herd can be disconcerting for your staff. It can be disconcerting for you too.

Some of your staff might feel abandoned, and many will feel fear and uncertainty. These are natural feelings, and anticipating them when you start your enterprise is valuable.

There will be a compulsion for some people to leave, or at the very least to look around for other opportunities, when you announce your intention to sell. Do not for one minute assume you can spring this as a surprise on your staff. They will know when you begin negotiating to sell, probably within days or weeks of your first serious courting of buyers. When you embark on the process of selling (which can take many months), trust becomes your ally in retaining staff, so prepare for openness. But even with transparency and your best attempts at gaining trust, expect some loss of staff.

It's important then, with this expected attrition, to avoid Key Person risks. Key Person risks occur when the value of your company becomes concentrated around one or two or a small handful of individuals.

Why am I bringing this up at this point, when you're mulling over the Exit Strategy but have not formed your company yet? Because thinking about this might help you structure your company to minimize this risk.

## *A dangerous lack of cohesion*

One of the more amazing consulting enterprises, in my view, is advertising. For sheer speed, creativity and volatility, I don't think there is any match. It must be the quintessential bucking bronco of consulting. Long before Mad Men was a television success, I knew an advertising executive. Nick had his own successful firm. I was fascinated by his enterprise model, which was spearheaded by very creative people in General Manager roles. It seemed to succeed in an unstructured way, and I was curious to know how. I learned that the three Creative Directors in his firm were the constantly sung heroes; the other fifty or so staff were not. The Creative Directors would find ideas that were often breathtaking, and the others would painstakingly turn those ideas into wonderful campaigns.

I observed, with some concern, that his enterprise had developed a class system. There were four heroes (including my friend), and then there were The Others. The four heroes landed lucrative contracts. They were prominent in the organization, and The Others worked in the background. Although I did not know for sure, I sensed that the pay gap and the equity gap between the heroes and The Others was a wide one.

When my friend began processes to sell his firm, The Others began to leave. One by one, then small group by small group. My friend made an attempt to introduce a new equity model, and succeeded in stemming the flow of his valuable employees, the ones who turned ideas into TV and magazine campaigns. But he had lost a noticeable percentage, and the sale negotiation process seemed more protracted. He sold his firm, successfully, in the end, at a lower price than he had hoped for. And he came very close to stranding his vision in an unwittingly-created class war.

## The cell model

One effective way to manage this Key Person risk is to take a page out of a terrorist handbook. If that sounds politically incorrect, I apologize. But let's learn lessons where we can find them, and let's not ignore them because of their origins. CNN and BBC World News teach us that terrorist organizations work in cells. If you remove one cell, the organization still functions, because it can continue to perform its activity unimpeded, and with relatively little loss of institutional capability. The cells should be of similar potency to each other (or, in the case of your consulting empire, of similar value to each other, insofar as this is practical). The more cells you have with similar potency, the more resilient your enterprise is to the loss of one or two cells.

We'll deal with this concept more as we look at some business planning.

You can 'anchor' your cells better, and further reduce attrition risk, by providing equity to the leaders of your cells well before selling. Why does this work? Quite simply, the acquiring firm sees an upside to the value in buying your company. That means Heavy Hitters Inc. believes that its investment might be doubled or tripled in a few years (say five years). Any shareholders in your company should benefit to a similar degree from their shareholdings. The financial incentive for them to stay when you go can be powerful.

In addition to reducing attrition risk by spreading the risk concentration (via cells) and providing financial upside (share allocations), it is also important to avoid excessive culture shock.

Although there is genuine warmth about running your enterprise like a family business, the reality is that a larger company acquiring your company will probably have more impersonal systems and processes. They might have a more overt hierarchy, possibly even stronger governance, and possibly some centralized control. Anticipating these, and gently building your company so that your staff are not left with a sour feeling of dreaded anticipation at systems, governance and hierarchy helps prevent culture shock.

If you want to really culture-shock-proof your enterprise, have your cell leaders create systems and governance. Emulate the systems and governance processes of your key clients. Your staff will learn to work with client processes, and will learn to pick the best from the smorgasbord of processes that they are exposed to. And in building processes, they will own them and be much more wedded to them. Your enterprise wins in two ways here. Firstly, by emulating key client processes (particularly the larger companies' processes) it is likely that your staff will be much less daunted when Heavy Hitters Inc. flaunts its processes. If your staff has worked with BP's or GlaxoSmithKline's or Nestle's processes, they will not be daunted by a large or mid-tier consulting firm's processes. Secondly, you'll build strong professionalism in your enterprise, and you might even find a slight upward bump in your multiplier as a result.

There is, of course, more to Exit Strategies than this, and the remaining chapters deal with them. But the main lesson for this Chapter is this: with nothing in place, with no functioning business and just the wisp of an idea in your head, don't feel sheepish about thinking in detail about your Exit Strategy. It will change how you think about your enterprise, and your wisp of a good idea will grow into a behemoth of a great vision. It won't do that overnight, like some Jack-and-the-Beanstalk sorcery, but it will grow. And the more time you spend on it, the more surely it will grow. Be patient, grasshopper, and don't start your story until you know the ending intimately.

## THREE TIPS

*Tip one*: Work out the capital value of your exit, and be prepared to recalculate it several times. Be clear about what you want your life to look like after you've achieved the sale and exit, because this vision – and not the dollar amount – is what will continue to inspire you.

*Tip two*: Be clear about how you will become redundant at the point of exit. It's easy to become tongue-in-cheek about this topic. Don't. Take your exit position very seriously, try to make yourself redundant, or be prepared for a golden handcuff clause in your sale contract.

*Tip three*: Think through your shareholding options at exit in a way that maximizes enterprise value through the retention of key staff.

## CHAPTER 3
# FINDING CONSULTANTS

*The best way to find yourself is to lose yourself*
*in the service of others.*
*– Mahatma Gandhi*

## Typecasting consultants

Consulting is a service industry. Don't let anyone ever tell you differently. And if you think it's anything else, don't try to create a consulting enterprise, because you would have started the journey with your shoelaces tied together.

Consulting is a service industry and its brand value comes from goodwill. The goodwill comes from customer satisfaction. The customer satisfaction comes not just from the outcome, but also from the customer's experience in reaching the outcome.

Consulting isn't service to humanity – in many cases it's far from it – but it is service nonetheless.

Good service requires humility, and herein lies the conundrum. You see, consultants solve problems (well, good consultants do, anyway). To solve some of the problems that you, as a consultant, are faced with, you'll need to have some special skills. After all, if just *anyone* could solve the problem at hand, no-one would call you, right? So you're quite good at what you do. Of course you are. Try being good at what you do, getting paid lots of money for solving problems that other mortals struggle with, and hanging onto humility. It's hard. The loss of humility is collateral damage. This is why the consulting world seems to be populated by arrogant and condescending individuals. Being a top-gun, humble consultant is a contradiction in terms.

But the conundrum gets worse. Try doing all that in a competitive environment where other smart people do what you do. You're going to wilt unless you have an ego the size of Africa. Why? Because you have to convince your prospective client that your special skills are simply more impressive than the other consultant's special skills. Remember, you don't always know what the answer to the client's problem is. But you need to have enough mojo to impress your client that you'll probably find an answer, better and faster, than the other consultant. You'll need confidence. So you're good at what you do, you are confident, and you need to hang on to humility. Talk about an attitude tightrope.

Look around for the consultant with humility; the one who's confident and good at what he or she does, and yet understands what good service looks like. There aren't that many of them. You conclude, quite correctly, that those who do walk the attitude tightrope can persist with their consulting career. But you're not here just to *persist*, you're here to build a consulting empire. So you need the confidence/humility cocktail and you need more.

A consultant's ego is a weapon of choice, and something to be nurtured. Muhammad Ali's ego set him up for greatness. He just didn't believe he'd be average. Usain Bolt didn't contemplate being the second fastest man alive; his ego told him he'd be the fastest man alive.

I've never done a controlled experiment on smart people, so the following is just a theory. But I have worked in government, and I've seen lots of smart people there. I've worked in industry – in multinationals – and I've seen lots of smart people there. I've worked in academia, and there are lots of smart people there. I've worked in consulting, and I see lots of smart people there too. But my overall sense is that I'll find more genuinely smarter people in consulting (as a percentage of all the people in consulting) than the other sectors. You can be unintelligent and make a decent career in government (you know that's true!) and in multinational corporations (that's definitely true). You can't pull it off in academia – you do need to be smart to get anywhere in academia – but you can be smart and ponderous, and you'll do just fine. But in consulting you need to be smart and quick. And it's not just about IQ and speed. It's also about EQ – emotional quotient – to underpin the service mentality. You need IQ and EQ to be a gun consultant.

EQ allows you to read your clients and your staff. It allows you to not just provide a good consulting service, but to make the experience for clients and staff engaging and positive.

Overall then, to be a good consultant you need IQ, EQ, ego and a service mentality. It also helps to know what you're doing, but lots of consultants do get away without that prerequisite!

So you need to ask yourself two questions. Are you consultant material? And, in building your consulting enterprise, can you find enough consulting-material types? Only you can answer the first, and the answer to the second is absolutely yes, provided you can answer the first with a yes.

*Growing and Selling a Successful Consulting Firm*

Why have I made such a big deal about the service mentality, and that balance between ego and humility? There are two things you can be sure of. One is that your consulting staff will follow your lead. They will watch you and emulate you. So this balance needs to ooze from your very pores. (Now you're asking the same question again…. why?… but I'm guessing with a touch of exasperation). So let me give you the second reason. If your staff haven't got the service mentality down pat, you *will* – and there is no doubt in my mind about this – spend huge amounts of your precious time smoothing over gradually worsening client relationships.

Client relationships, as we'll discuss later, are important. Very important. Critical, in fact. And I'm still understating this issue because I haven't found words strong enough to convey this aspect. To build a consulting empire efficiently, you need particularly good client relationships. When I say *efficiently*, I mean this: if you want to build a consulting empire and not age like you're maturing in dog years, get the relationships right, and get your staff to get them right. It's no fun to be a thirty- or forty-something millionaire and look like you're seventy, with bad ulcers and a wonky heart.

There is an often-quoted statistic that goes like this. It takes four times as much expense and effort to find a new client as it does to keep existing clients. Some statistics use 'ten' instead of 'four', but the number is largely irrelevant. It's just bad business to have client turnover that you can attribute to average or poor service. Some people call this 'client churn' (which sounds painful for the clients but is actually far more painful for the consultants).

## The disappointed client

*When I was selling my first consulting practice, a new Managing Director was running the show and I was tidying up paperwork with the Exit sign figuratively strapped to my chest. Dreams of a long holiday on a deserted island ran through my head whether I was asleep or awake. I was a largely useless cog in our machine, having made myself mostly redundant over the previous couple of years. Our clients knew I was leaving.*

*I had a long distance call that awoke me at 3am. One minute I was strumming a guitar on a cliff overlooking a half-moon beach and listening to the surf beat its eternal, soothing metronome. Then my guitar playing became stilted and tuneless. Just one chord in an annoying two-beat shrill. Drring-drring. Drring-drriing. I woke up very unhappy about my interrupted dream, and picked up the phone.*

*It was a valued client we had had for almost six years, calling from many time zones away, where we had a large consulting project with the company he worked for. When he realized where in the world I was, and what time it was for me, he offered to call later. But I was awake, and I asked him what was up.*

*I regretted answering the phone, let alone asking him that question, as for the next twenty minutes he recounted the way his project was 'unraveling'. It wasn't, really. It had hit a couple of hurdles, which was not unexpected. What was really upsetting for him was that the service had 'deteriorated'. And he was frustrated and angry.*

*There was nothing I could do, other than suggest he approach the new Managing Director to walk him step by step through the hurdles and what was being done. I told him I had no authority to address the things he thought needed fixing. I gave him a sympathetic ear and not much else. Privately I thought the problems and the solutions being applied matched well, and my previous staff were applying the same intellectual rigor as ever before. But something had changed in the way they communicated with and empathized with clients – or this client at least.*

*After the call, as I tried to get back to sleep and find that elusive cliff-top and beach again, I reflected over two things. One was how easy it is to change a company's service mentality for the worse, in just a few short months, if the service mentality is not being lived by senior management. People follow the cues. Senior management provides the cues.*

*The other was how grief-stricken a client could be when the service that he or she enjoyed before disappeared. It's the reason a client stays with a company with great service, even when other consulting firms are wining and dining potential clients to excess, even when the others are providing introductions to senior Ministers and publishing their works in the Harvard Business Review. It's the reason we grew so dramatically and confidently. Clients value the quality of service, and this service protects you in a highly competitive environment. It can't be faked, and it takes hard work to maintain as a culture.*

*Less than six months later, after a long and faithful association with our consulting firm, this client went to another consulting firm.*

## Four types of consultants

When I think of *valuable* consultants, I think of four categories; hunters, farmers, creatives and closers. These are not mutually exclusive categories, and I'll show you how they feature in your consulting empire.

The hunter is the glamor-puss of consulting. He or she wins clients through great business development and through finding the value proposition that the client has not had before. The hunters have a competitive edge that keeps them hungry. They are the high-fivers of your empire, and their ego is extremely well developed. They find gratification in the hunt and the win (or the 'kill', as some of them will actually call it!). They see themselves at the top of the food chain, and you will often hear them pointing out (usually during salary and bonus reviews) that if not for them, the company would have no clients.

The farmer is a lot less conspicuous. He or she guides the clients through their problems and their solutions. The farmer is there every day, with both the mundane and the exciting parts of the assignments, a constant in the ebb and flow of the relationship that might see difficult days. Farmers delight in elegant solutions and in a job well done; they see beauty in well-oiled machinery. They worry if the assignment is less profitable than it should be. Farmers are the stewards of your consulting empire, and they often do not see it, overshadowed as they are by their A-lister hunters.

Creatives are your smart problem-solvers. They live for the unique solutions to the rare and difficult problems. They work best in complexity. Sometimes they will look for a complicated solution when a simple one stares them in the face. They are usually at the cutting edge of knowledge, a position they keep through the sheer force of their own thirst for creative power. Creatives come in all shapes and sizes, from the antisocial tech-nerd to the extroverted one with the slight behavioral problem. Their Achilles' heel is their tendency to boredom. Once they see the solution, they develop ADD.

Closers get the job done. They will slog. If success is twenty percent inspiration and eighty percent perspiration, meet the sweaty guys.

They have focus, and an almost unbreakable thousand-yard stare for the finish line. They have tenacity and an uncanny ability to stretch time, creating great final products under intense schedule pressures. They are the engine of your well-oiled machinery, marathon runners rather than sprinters, both efficient and effective. Every closer you have can probably go out into the market on their own and make a successful solo career or small business in consulting. Simply because they get the job done. They have no Achilles' heel.

If you map your types out on a two by two grid, you'll find consultants group like this.

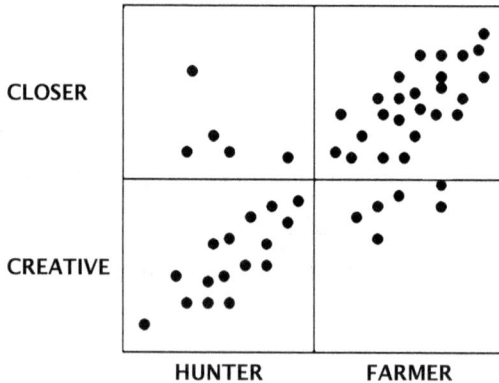

CLOSER

CREATIVE

HUNTER    FARMER

Creative-hunters are your business development agents who often flourish in the private-sector client world, finding competitive edges and winning work prolifically. They find new business and new clients. Closer-farmers are your client stewards, delivering the work no matter where the work is won (from the private sector or the public sector). They get repeat business from their clients. Creative-farmers and closer-hunters are thinner on the ground. Creative-farmers are good at finding cross-marketing opportunities within existing client organizations. They can leverage good service to widen the scope of activity within a given client organization. Closer-hunters are what

I euphemistically call tender-jockeys. Don't worry, it's a term of endearment. Closer-hunters are particularly good at finding competitive edges in public tenders, where tenacity and strategic thinking are needed in roughly equal measure.

When you start your consulting empire, you need to play all four roles of hunter, farmer, creative and closer. It's a busy period of your life, because all four hats are difficult to wear simultaneously. As your empire grows, you find 'specialists' that fall into these categories. Your ability to recognize them for what they are, and what they can be, will be one of your leadership attributes that will help create a successful consulting practice.

Are these all the types of consultants that are available? No. You will find people that are neither hunters nor farmers. And they may be neither creatives nor closers. They are useful members of your consulting organization, but they are like worker bees. They are reasonably disposable, and easily replaceable. I once said that to my HR manager, who was understandably shocked at my seemingly cavalier attitude to this cadre of my staff, and roundly chastised me for using these terms in front of her. Actually, she chastised me for thinking that way at all (I'm sheepish to admit I was immature enough to use the word *filler* as well, but that was largely to goad her). I was really just being pragmatic, if a little politically incorrect. In building a successful consulting practice – just like building a house – you need to know your materials. You need to know what materials have special properties and are a little bit rare, and you need to source them differently, store them differently, and look after them differently. You need to know what materials are plentiful, where they fit in your structure, and be aware that they can be procured easily. You treat all your staff with respect but you must learn to differentiate between consulting talents.

*Growing and Selling a Successful Consulting Firm*

### The dangers of non-delivery

David, a professional associate of many years, was the MD of a large and well-known project management organization. He remunerated staff extremely well on the basis of new sales, and not particularly for much else. It was an aggressive growth-oriented organization and it stocked itself with a bunch of talented (and expensive) business development personnel. It also stocked itself with 'filler' material to complete consulting assignments; they were sometimes referred to as worker bees by senior management. Its emphasis on new clients and new sales worked well initially in each office. Lots of work was won. Lots of work was done. And while it was done professionally, it wasn't done at much above an average level of competence; not brilliance – and not really with a lot of client empathy.

The firm became known among clients for making promises it never quite delivered on. The sales pitches were magnificent, and the delivery was average. For a while, the offices grew quickly, but with a notably high turnover of clients. I remember looking at the client lists for the twenty highest revenue sources for two back-to-back years, country by country, and being struck by how different they were in almost every country. Hardly any clients from the first year's list were on the second year's list, and it was a systematic characteristic.

Many offices stalled, and the offices in smaller cities had an unnerving habit of closing down after a few years, or being heavily subsidized by other parts of the business. They simply ran out of clients in their catchment. Eventually, too many clients came to believe that the firm made magnificent sales pitches followed by average delivery, and they simply shopped around more for the services they needed. The consulting offices cut their prices to entice more clients, which worked to some degree but also helped to commoditize and depress the consulting market in their *areas. Barriers to entry were low for other consulting firms wishing to enter the market or increase market share. Cutting prices below a sustainable level is never a good thing; clients and customers win in the short term, and everyone loses in the long term. You can't then hold onto those expensive business development types, and you begin a downward spiral. Those less successful offices commanded a sizeable part of senior management time during their subsidized years as they tried to navigate their way out of an accelerating decline.*

*The organization survived with a reasonable, but not particularly exciting, rate of return. I'm not saying you're doomed to failure if you get this mix of consultants and drivers wrong, I'm just saying you're inefficient. In this case, the organization survived because it was big enough that large client companies requiring large-scale projects to be carried out across many parts of the country (such as wholesale acquisitions) really had no other choice. But I often wondered at how much more it could have flourished if it had stocked itself differently with people, and with more strategy and purpose. I wondered how different it might have been if hunters and farmers were equitably honored for their places in the organization, and if the ratio of creatives to closers was carefully geared to increase client retention.*

## Making and nourishing your matrix

In finding consultants for your organization, your first and last thoughts, sandwiching your strategy, should be that you are investing in people. Every dollar you earn is earned because people are using their minds enthusiastically, and that's the energy your consulting organization should create and harness.

So what's your leadership trait in creating your consulting empire? If anything, it's understanding people and motivating them. In that way it's no different to any other organization; a manufacturing firm or a bank or a retail organization. You'll hear CEOs say that all the time. The leadership trait of understanding people is probably *more* critical in a consulting firm, largely because people make up about 100% of your assets. But sadly, most consulting firms fail to recognize this.

Most of the compliments you receive about your consulting firm will be about your people. "Nick really delivered that project", or "Maria worked around the country risk area brilliantly." When you hear that enough times, it sinks in that your people make you successful.

But your consulting empire is unlikely to be a flat structure, and you want to propagate your appreciation of the value of people through the organization, below your great managers and below their people, all the way to the humble vacation student you employ. There are two very good reasons to do this. One reason is to do with success. If you invest in making your key people good hunters and good farmers, and you get that balance right, you'll attract and retain clients, and your workload will grow. And if your workload grows, it creates the second reason. You want to attract good people into your company so that you *can* grow.

Like any profession, consultants talk. They know which companies are good to work for, which ones are successful and which ones are sweatshops. Remember what we talked about at the start of this chapter? Consultants have big egos. Consultants like belonging to clubs of great consultants. I can only recall a handful of times when my companies needed to advertise to recruit staff. This was typically at the start of a new office in a new country. After that, if we got the people culture right, and the right ratios of farmers and hunters, we had no shortage of applicants for roles in our firm. It wasn't a recession either; in several of those countries unemployment was at low levels. But we frequently had people from other firms asking if they could join our firm. People talk.

Investing in people in consulting, it seems, can be a bit of a perpetual motion machine. You think carefully about whom you hire and you invest in those people. You treat people like precious materials with which to build your firm. You find a balance between challenge and reward, between work and play; one that creates a consulting culture of your choosing. Create a work hard, play hard culture where hunters and farmers and creative and closers feel highly valued. It's a very energetic environment. You may have more hunters than farmers as you break into new markets. Or you may have more farmers than hunters because you have a low client turnover rate (or high repeat work). Whatever the mix is, make sure it's a deliberate mix and not an accidental one. Celebrate repeat work as well as new clients, signaling strongly that both farmers and hunters are valued in your company.

At any time in your company's life, you should have a view of what type of people your company will need in the next little while (I typically use a one-year forward-looking window to "bracket" my next recruitment mix). There isn't a formula; many factors are at play, including your own delivery and growth strategy. Are you diversifying your services, or consolidating them, or improving them? If you are expanding, do you need to regroup the way you manage your company? What types of people are on the market? And of course, many of these questions come with a context that is dependent on external factors, including the state of the economy, growth and decline in sectors and services, the shape of the labor market and so on. But regardless of what these factors are, if you don't have a well formed view on the mix you're working towards, you are not building an outstanding consulting firm. You're simply putting bums on seats, and that is one way of commoditizing your firm. I call it commoditization by apathy, and that apathy is yours to tolerate or eliminate.

### The wall builder

*On one of my consulting assignments in China, I had one of those mystic Kung Fu experiences. I was stranded in a remote area for two days while waiting for a charter flight that had, unfortunately, developed engine trouble and was being repaired at its originating airport. For part of the second day, I had no laptop battery left, and my phone battery was down to less than 10%, so I sat under a tree, wrote a little bit in my notebook, and generally watched the ambling pace of life in the countryside. I watched a farmer building a wall out of stones. He wasn't using cement, so he was relying on the 'fit' of the stones to generate his structural stability. He first spent a lot of time gathering stones, and he placed them in three piles; larger angular stones, smaller angular stones and smoother or rounder stones of all sizes. Only after the piles were quite large did he begin with the wall. His selection of each stone was deliberate, and he chose painstakingly from each pile, sometimes testing the fit of a stone and then rejecting it for that placement, putting it back in the pile he had taken it from. As the piles diminished, he wandered off and began collecting stones again, until the piles were of a healthy size, and then he began stacking the wall once more. The second time he wandered off, I innocently sauntered over to his wall and looked at it more closely. It was packed tightly and looked surprisingly strong.*

*In my view, the Chinese farmer used the same type of foresight needed to build a good – or great – consulting firm. The piles of stones he collected represented the type of market intelligence needed to identify the pool of employees, and each pile represented a different type of consultant. His choice of placement began with a strong foundation, and every stone he placed in the wall added to or maintained that strength. If it didn't do either of those things, he put it back in the pile. He kept going back to the market and understanding what was available, pre-selecting his future stock. It might have taken him a bit longer to build that wall, but it wasn't going to give way under stress. It was a good wall.*

## Take the time to choose wisely

How much time do you spend in selecting your staff? In my view, the more time you spend, the better you'll build your firm. In theory, there is probably a point of diminishing return, when the extra benefit you create is small compared to the amount of time and energy you spend. I don't think I found that point, and I always felt that there weren't enough hours in the day to devote to this activity. In hindsight, I would have spent more on it if I could have found a way to do it.

## THREE TIPS

*Tip one*: Segment your consultants (farmers, hunters, etc.) in your mind, and plan for how you stock those segments to fit your consulting model.

*Tip two*: Set up your salary schemes to be attractive and incentivized; remember, if you're the new kid on the block, you carry a risk premium because you haven't proven yourself to be a sustainable enterprise.

*Tip three*: If you intend to grow, never, *ever* stop looking voraciously for talent.

# CHAPTER 4
# KEEPING CONSULTANTS

*It is best not to swap horses when crossing the river*
*– Abraham Lincoln*

## Attracting your staff

Consulting is a highly competitive industry, which breeds competitive participants. Consulting firms poach staff from each other all the time. And consultants are used to looking for bigger, brighter and better outcomes, so they look around for employment opportunities. It's surprisingly easy to lose staff to the public or private industry sectors, or to other consulting firms. I have found potential staff turnover levels in consulting firms to be higher than in other sectors. It's reasonably simple, I think, to figure out why this might be so.

Firstly, consultants tend to have healthy egos, which means they like to feel valued and important. They preen a lot. If the employer (you) represents a mirror, it needs to be a flattering mirror. Like Snow White's nemesis and her magic mirror, when a consultant asks "who's the smartest/most creative/most profitable of them all?" the mirror needs to be prepared to give credit where credit is due, and be slightly effusive about it. False flattery is, of course, dangerous and not something I'd advise. But flattery where it's due – when you have a good consultant of course – is an essential part of keeping your people. These healthy egos make consultants susceptible to the seduction of other consulting firms.

In building your own firm, you'll spend some time luring consultants away from their existing jobs. My hiring tactics were simple, but very effective. I would acknowledge what the consultant (my prospective employee) was good at, and remark on how those strengths could be utilized for even greater things. To be precise, greater things in *my* firm.

Greater challenge, greater reward and greater profile are the three things good consultants hunger for, and you need to be prepared to configure your organization to offer these. If you achieve the potential for rapid growth, which is typically when you win more work than you can handle, your organization has to be primed to attract people. If you work on priming your organization to attract people *after* you win projects, you create a delay. The incoming work suffers while you warm up your recruitment profile, and you miss the opportunity to 'surf the wave' into a permanent growth mode.

## Engaging your staff

Once hired though, keeping your staff engaged is important. Note, I didn't say they had to be happy; but of course they shouldn't be unhappy. If you try to please everyone, you won't manage it, you'll look like a weak leader and you will end up with anarchy. But keeping a good consultant's mind engaged is essential to hanging on to him or her, to developing the person, and to set the right scene for that person to want to be a leader in your firm.

This is actually easier to do than most people realize, although it is time-consuming. The engagement takes several forms, and you look for the opportunities where they lie. It is easier if you are watchful for these opportunities, and much harder if you spend time pondering how to create them. I'll explain some in the next few pages.

When you start and run your own firm, the processes and structures you need to manage the growing workload and the increasing number of people are many. The latent trap is that you think that you'll have to solve all these challenges – for example, create administrative or project management processes – so that your staff would be free to get on with what they were doing. There is certainly some truth to the notion, as smooth processes lead to efficiency, which invariably leads to higher profit margins. Also, if you don't have them, the troops can get frustrated and demoralized. But does it matter who creates these processes? Actually, it does.

Budding leaders are hungry for a challenge, and they pounce on such problems ravenously when offered them. The chance to develop processes in a growing company is exciting to many, and it's engaging for them to do this work. Certainly, you might have the benefit of experience and can offer sage advice from time to time, but you may find your staff members are far more creative than you at finding processes that work for them. There might be the invariable tension of your expectations of rigor versus their expectations of ease of application, but this is a healthy tension and it adds to engagement to have a healthy debate with the boss.

Remember, many staff members appreciate being given the responsibility of creating good processes. They might even enjoy the opportunity to debate the philosophical and practical aspects of these processes with you, their leader.

*Growing and Selling a Successful Consulting Firm*

The process review sessions can be enjoyable, despite some of the dry administrative topics you might discuss. Make them engaging and fun. The trick to doing this is to anticipate well in advance when a process will be needed, and start the work early. Remove the urgency from the task, and allow creativity to blossom. A mining company I worked at often held the process review sessions in the boardroom at the end of a week, beer or wine in hand, the staff presenting their approach and where they had got to, seeking feedback. I used this tactic in my own firms, because I saw it worked. In time, you notice that your people *own* your firm's evolution. They have a more personal connection to how the business is growing and maturing. Remember your Exit Strategy?

Problem-solving sessions can also be very engaging. Often, consultants pride themselves on tackling difficult assignments and breaking new ground. Note that you can't make all of your work about challenges and breaking new ground; there will and should always be a majority that you might call your bread-and-butter work. The bread-and-butter work brings in the money, but your unique signature as a consultant can be found in the challenging areas you choose to tackle.

Not everyone works on challenging projects all the time. In fact, less than twenty percent of your staff actually might, at any one time. But the problem solving sessions can be an open forum for the twenty percent of the staff working on challenging projects at the time to present to the others the problem that was confounding them, and for the others to offer up solutions. When you run these, two useful rules are (a) that all ideas are documented, and (b) that there is no such thing as a dumb idea. In my first consulting foray, many of our problem solving sessions, again usually held late in the day on a Thursday or Friday, stretched into dinners out or pizzas ordered in. I recall there was lots of laughter at these sessions, and some very good ideas. My recollection is that the ideas got more creative and less practical after a certain point (correlated somewhat to the amount of beer or wine consumed), and eventually evaporated into a mist of camaraderie. But more often than not, there were good conversations that sparked good ideas the following week or the following month. I think of these ideas as bonuses. The idea of the problem-solving sessions is to engage, not actually find solutions. Importantly, it helps dissipate the silos that can creep into your organization, especially when you configure your firm as a collection of 'cells'.

## Teaming your cells

Connecting social interaction with success is a powerful engagement tool. Everyone does it; the celebratory lunch or drinks or speech and champagne when some important milestone is reached. You can go one better if you frequently celebrate continuous success. For example, one of my offices had a *Party Accrual Fund*, where a small percentage of the profit for the month was set aside each month, with a modest jackpot for successive months where profit targets were met. Every quarter, the youngest four people in the office would be charged with determining how to spend the money. There were only a couple of rules. One was that no more than 25% of the money could be spent on alcohol (a commitment to responsible drinking!). Another was that staff would need to find creative, inclusive ways of celebrating as an office. Obviously, this type of fund can get quite skinny if you have a quiet quarter, but again the point of the exercise is not entirely about how big the party is. In the case of that particular office, the point of the exercise was to engage the youngest staff, for the more seasoned staff to enjoy the fruits of their creativity, and of course to link social camaraderie with success without your shadow, as the leader, being cast over it too much.

There are many other ways to engage your staff and build your own culture. Over time, I've found that creativity is virtually boundless. The reality is that there is a deep well of opportunity for keeping staff engaged, and you are unlikely to run out of options if you are genuinely determined to keep looking down this well.

Other engaging strategies are linked to progression in the organization. In consulting, client stewardship provides one of the stronger motivators for staff. The opportunity to become a client manager – a task usually reserved for talented 'farmers' or senior staff – and retain or increase their business serves as an attractive 'coming of age' honor to many maturing staff.

All of these add value to an organization's culture, provided the initiatives are varied (not everyone is engaged by the same thing), they do not exclude people, there is a sense of fairness and transparency, and they are integrated into everyday activities more than the obvious momentous events. But the single most valuable thing to do, and all good leaders know this, is to lead your firm by walking around. When you start a small firm, you will know everyone you hired, and you will be the patriarch or matriarch. There is an amazing amount of appreciation that staff hold for you, when you spare five or ten minutes to discuss work, how they are going, recent events, future plans… virtually anything that allows them to see your passion for the company. Too many entrepreneurs fall into the trap of becoming too busy to do this. Many try to save money on administrative tasks, and to things like invoicing themselves. Others adopt a control-and-secrecy approach about how 'their' company runs, and resist the delegation of tasks to others. You, the leader, have the power to hire whomever you need to undertake the tasks you need to delegate in order to spend time walking around, looking and talking, sensing, processing, engaging, and shaping your company culture.

Everything mentioned so far about engagement contributes to company culture. Vision and mission statements, and shared values, contribute to company culture. The way your PA interacts with your staff contributes to company culture. Your human resource processes contribute to your company culture. In fact, it's hard to find much that doesn't contribute to company culture. And this is very important to note.

Assume *everything* contributes to company culture. If you know what you *don't* want in your company culture, focus relentlessly on avoiding, rejecting and eliminating these things. Don't condone the behaviors that might lead to unwanted characteristics of your company culture. You can be quite a Nazi in this area and get away with it, provided you are doing enough positive things contributing to company culture. If you don't have this balance – if you are all about avoidance, rejection and elimination – your company will feel sterile and controlled. Rules are necessary, but so are positive affirmations, and the latter can be much more powerful.

### Creating cultures

*A growing environmental firm began to think about its culture about a year or so after it was created. The owner tried to be more definitive about the company culture she wanted. Although she was in her forties, it was becoming clear to Helen that her focus on creative solutions to unique problems fitted a certain age demographic. Employees with eight to fifteen years' experience had agile minds, they had not become set in their ways, and they were hungry for fame and success. They were also getting married or having babies.*

*Helen decided to become much more family friendly. However, she did not want to lose the edge that she had, which was a powerful work ethic; one that had served her well. She decided to combine the family-friendly platform with a work hard, play hard culture, and a don't-do-like-I-say-do-like-I-do mantra. None of this was Machiavellian, she insisted, nor could it be classified as social engineering.*

*She remarked that by the time a year had passed, she could see a difference. She really liked the culture that emerged, and noted that it was energized from within. Tight-knit offices were formed, and there was a slight edge of elitism, which is distinctly not a liability in a consulting firm. Successes were celebrated and failures were despised for the palpable embarrassment they created. If her firm lost a prospect, she would be philosophical about it, but she reported that her staff seemed to take it more personally.*

*"It was like having over-achieving children," she said. "The family-friendly work-hard ethic seemed to make people more fiercely protective of their success. It was as if they wanted the model to work for me, because it worked for them personally."*

*Years later, this observation held me in good stead when I started my own firm.*

## A word on culture

There isn't a 'right' culture. There is one that you are comfortable with, that supports your Exit Strategy and makes the journey to that exit fulfilling. It helps to understand the self-reinforcing aspects of culture and how they cement the total culture into place. It helps to know what culture you want and why, and it is essential to know what culture you *don't* want. And it's vitally important you know that where you land is going to keep your best people.

### Acknowledging good work

*As a 'new' entrant in a crowded consulting world, working the conferences and networking hard, I often ran into other owners or consulting companies and – after some cagey conversations where we would each would 'feel out' the competition – we would chat about common challenges such as creating a company culture.*

*At a mining conference in Melbourne, Australia, I recall talking fondly about our staff culture to the MD of another consulting firm. I mentioned that I had a discipline of knowing who was doing what in the company (we only had around fifty employees in two countries at the time, so it was possible for me to know everyone reasonably well). I explained that just the other week, after an employee had worked hard and well for a few months in delivering a project for a client, I had insisted he go away somewhere for a week with his wife and young son. We had no time-in-lieu policy (I had felt that meticulously accounting 'overtime' led to a culture I did not want) but it was suggested the leave was not to be deducted from the employee's holiday bank. We gave him a generous budget that would allow him to acquire a high-rise apartment on the beach for a week, and asked that he send us the bill to pay.*

*The MD looked at me like I was soft in the head. "Dangerous precedent," he remarked, one eyebrow raised in mild incredulity. Clearly he thought I was not long for this consulting world.*

*I didn't explain myself, but cheerfully regaled him with another story of our first maternal leave experience. A senior manager and I visited* our employee at her home when she was four months pregnant and after some discussion, organized a desk, computer and air conditioning for a spare room, and took her shopping for an ergonomic chair that suited her increasingly pregnant frame. We insisted that she work from home rather than commute – for the rest of her pregnancy. The gesture came with no expectations or conditions. For all we knew, motherhood could re-prioritize her life and she may never return to work.

The MD, whose intent it was to mingle with and network with people who could be of use to him in the future, decided right there that I would not be one of those, because I was clearly destined for the poorhouse. He probably made a mental note to avoid hiring me when I came around begging for a job. With a sympathetic smile, he excused himself and left.

From a monetary perspective, what I had described were minor investments, even if the MD had thought we were being wasteful. What made them impactful was that they were personalized. Each employee we treated this way soon forgets the monetary value of what you do. They remember that it was a personal investment in their wellbeing. It is the difference between sending a check for Christmas and finding, for a similar amount, a gift that is truly appreciated.

The maternity leave employee returned to work after a year off, and became loyal to a fault. Her work wasn't just good; it was often inspired. She talked about her ergonomic maternity chair for months after she returned to work, which was some eighteen months after our shopping spree. She giggled while describing how we had spent an afternoon shopping for and trying out chair after chair, our patient frozen grins in place while she lolled about and squeaked delightedly when she found a particularly gimmicky chair. It was such a small thing, and it was disconcerting to me (and others, I'm sure) how she could think the story could

*be even remotely captivating to anyone, but there it was. Her enthusiasm*
*for our company was infectious, and four years later she had person-*
*ally talked three talented individuals into joining us from other firms.*
*Of course it wasn't just about one chair, we did these things often enough*
*that they were part of the culture, but not so often that they became an*
*expectation. But culture is won in inches, not in yards, and many little*
*things go into weaving a cultural fabric.*

## Remuneration

Remuneration is, of course, an obvious way to retain staff. In the
startup phase, remuneration can be a large hurdle. Anyone worth his
or her salt might place a risk premium on joining you, because you're
new and untested. Sure, your concept sounds good and you might be
gifted with genius salesmanship when it comes to recruitment. But in
your startup period, your coffers are not deep, and good people might
command higher than market rates.

It's important to understand market rates. The obvious reason is
that you want to pay in the right range. The less obvious reason, and in
my experience the more useful application of that knowledge, is that
you can create an incentive scheme that retains your best people. This
allows you to break the deadlock of negotiations that invariably seem
to exceed market salaries when you are small and your brand does not
attract the talent you want.

Some companies use the incentive scheme to reduce the basic salary of employees to say the bottom quartile of the market, or 5% below
the salary floor, and provide incentives for the best people to prosper. I
don't believe in tampering with the basic salary. In my experience, you
devalue your work-hard-play-hard culture if you try to 'save' on basic

salaries, and you project a penny-pinching image. You risk giving with one hand and taking away with the other. Instead, I believe in honoring basic market salary scales and provided bonus schemes and share incentives to create a more interesting upside.

If you are creative in your small enterprise, you'll find ways to dream up – and honor! – such interesting upsides. At the start, you (and any co-owners) own one hundred percent of the company, which invariably allows for small but significant share options to be offered to talented people without dilution. As you grow, dilution of shares becomes a possibility. If you grow internationally, foreign exchange rates create interesting options for cross-holding in shares between the different countries, which in my experience seems to be particularly attractive to people. All companies will have different breadths in latitude to be creative, but one of the lessons I learned in creating consulting firms was that you were generally pleasantly surprised at how much latitude there was if you applied a creative mind to it.

### Investing in others' dreams

*One of the issues that plagues employers is that gifted staff leave to pursue their dreams. Why? Because the potential for those dreams to come true does not exist where they are. It was an issue that I hadn't wrestled with when I first started my own enterprise, but I was vaguely aware I would need a strategy for this risk in the future.*

*Two consultants I knew had started their own venture some years ago, in logistics planning and management. They told me about one of their success stories. One of their employees was a talented financial analyst who had lost his job after a merger between his employer and another industrial company. They had offered him a job in consulting,* which he accepted. However, they knew that logistics planning was not something he really wanted to do, and that their company was too small for him. Their projects dealt in projects that had fewer zeroes on their balance sheets than he was used to. It felt, they said, like a placeholder and a backward step. Sooner or later, he would leave – and it would probably be sooner. But in the process of interviewing, and in the months after, they became aware that his secret dream was to be an entrepreneur, to develop his own company. So they created a small company focusing on economic evaluations. They gave him a 33% share of this new company, the MD role, and let him indulge his dream. Their systems became his, and so he was able to get up and running in a very short time. A few years later they sold the small company for a very useful profit.

They retained the employee for much longer than they should have, they benefitted from his wisdom in their ranks, and they created a profitable operating and capital asset. In the intervening years, he was offered lucrative CFO jobs in other companies. In retrospect, they said, the employee did far better for himself with the option they offered him, than he would have with the CFO offers, and he got to experience a dream that he had nurtured for years. It was a classic win-win outcome.

## The sustainability of honored values

At the start of your consulting journey, such initiatives might seem ridiculous, overly generous and most of all counter to conventional wisdom. But being shackled to conventional wisdom is an exercise in attaining an average outcome. By definition, you'll be like the others, plus or minus ten percent. If you want your people to stay with you, be different in a way that appeals to your people, and honor your own values. It's a potent mix that creates loyalty. And loyalty creates an energy in your ranks that is hard to define, harder to bottle and yet is palpably and undeniably present.

The premise, then, is simple. To keep the best people, you need a culture that attracts and retains smart, capable and egotistical people. The culture must be authentic, because falsehoods or pretending rots your culture from within. It needs to be based on values; values that you hold high, and that others will respect. It needs to be generous but not wasteful. It needs to be disciplined but not constricting. But whatever the values are, you need to be crystal clear in your own mind about them, and you need to honor them day after day. And one day, it becomes your sustainable culture.

## THREE TIPS

*Tip one*: Your culture is your greatest drawcard in keeping good consultants and encouraging those you don't want to leave. Be clear about what you want in your culture, and be even clearer about what you *don't* want.

*Tip two*: Focus on having your best people 'owning' your growth, systems and culture; they will be your greatest assets when you execute your exit strategy and they are more likely to be loyal to the enterprise they have helped shape.

*Tip three*: Be present. Walk around. For a very long time, you will be their touchstone. Stay available.

# CHAPTER 5

# DOING WHAT YOU DO

*Choose a job you love and you will never*
*have to work a day in your life*
*– Confucius*

## Building models

One of the benefits of starting your own consulting firm is that you can do what you want. One of the dangers of starting your own consulting firm is that you can do what you want. It's a volatile paradox; one that can blow up in your face.

If you are a lone consultant, a One-Person-Band, you can play exactly to your strengths. In fact, if there is a good market for your strengths (in other words if the demand exceeds the supply), it's sometimes wisest not to diversify. Your fee rate, or charge out rate, is directly proportional to the degree of difficulty of the specialized area you work in, and your expertise in that area. A rule of thumb is that you'll work less, for more money, if you can sustainably hold your charge out rate at a high level. And ideally, you'll turn down projects because you're too busy, the projects don't turn you on or frankly, you prefer to be sipping Mai Tais on a beach between June and August every year, and – what the hell – do the same in the southern hemisphere around December and January.

If you're building your consulting empire, it's harder to find that sweet spot. Many factors interfere with your prospects. Labor limitations are the most significant factor. It works like this. If you're famous for your skills at doing a particular type of consulting job – let's call it Heroic Consulting – you'll be in demand. So you hang out your shingle for Heroic Consulting and you go looking for other Heroic consultants to recruit into your band of entrepreneurs. Quite soon you discover there aren't many of these Heroic consultants around. If there were, they would be doing much the same as you are, and they wouldn't be working for you; they'd be working for themselves. If, by chance, there were lots of these Heroic consultants around, perhaps working for the big companies, then – hey presto – supply would be meeting demand, the niche fades away and eventually it ceases to exist.

So the concept that you can build a company of 100 people in Heroic Consulting mostly fails miserably. I'm sure there are exceptions to the rule, but I'm a firm believer in taking the carefully-calculated winning shot rather than hoping for a fluke. I would never cross my fingers and hope I can make that unlikely-to-succeed concept work for me.

Let's look at the 'build' of consulting firms.

One step up from the One-Person-Band model is the Small Niche Band. The Small-Niche-Band brings together a cadre of three, four or five understudies in Heroic consulting and, under your tutelage, forms into a potent Small-Niche consulting firm. You're still a long way off your dreams of a consulting empire, but you've evolved from a single-celled organism to a multi-celled organism which – as you'll recall your biology teacher telling you – is a pretty significant step up the evolutionary chain. You sense there is a domino effect that you can tap into.

Recall that, earlier in this book, the concept of 'cells' was mentioned. A cell is effectively a Small-Niche consulting firm. One catalyst for growth is to find cells that are complementary to each other. Cells that don't work in isolation; those that sit on some kind of value chain and 'knit' together to retain their individual value but still form part of a greater value bundle.

This requires an astonishing amount of thinking and planning. I won't pretend it's easy or quick. In fact, I'll stress it again. Don't stop scheming about your cell model, not even after your months of planning have resulted in something that looks achievable, not even while you're achieving it three years later, not even when it looks like you've achieved it six years later. Every cell you add to this value chain of Small-Niche-Bands integrates value into your company. If you want to enjoy everything the company does, you'll feel like avoiding the 'boring' or 'unsexy' skills. And if you choose to indulge this whim, you make your job much more complex. Remember the Chinese farmer and my Kung Fu experience? You need small round stones and big craggy ones to make a strong wall.

There is an often-unsung benefit to getting your portfolio of Small-Niche-Bands right. Industry seems to operate in cycles. There are boom times and slow times. International markets change the prospects of bigger clients, and national economies vary the prospects of smaller clients. Your clients' prospects affect yours, and quite directly. In some years, by mirroring changes to the industrial landscape around you, a handful of your cells will prosper while others might struggle. In other years, other cells prosper while previously lucrative cells might struggle. And while you might optimistically hope that none of your cells will ever struggle, to borrow a wise phrase, *hope for the best and plan for the worst*. Think of your portfolio of Small-Niche-Bands as a diversified strategy in motion. The diversification potentially makes you more resilient to the fickleness of markets.

So that's the theory. Does it work in practice? I found that, like most things in life, the answer was not "yes" or "no", but "more yes than no". And the reason that it's not an unqualified "yes" is that you would have to be able to see the future of the market economies and operating models of your clients to get that answer. And if you could, you wouldn't start a consulting firm, you'd play the stock market from your smartphone on a beach in the Seychelles.

Given yours and my frustrating incompetence in reading the future accurately, the trick is putting knowledge into practice so that the answer does actually turn out to be "more yes than no".

Remember, the market fluctuations than occur and influence industries around you are outside of your control. You can only watch and marvel at boom-and-bust cycles. But the market fluctuations, and their influence on the industries around you, are not out of reach of your *understanding*. I found that was where I would discover how to make my answer "more yes than no". To apply your understanding to the challenge of which cells to develop, look at supply and demand separately, then together – for each cell, for each cluster of cells, and for your whole organization.

## Connecting sectors and services

Large consulting firms often model their activities around two axes. One axis is "services", which is essentially supply. The other is "sectors", which is where your demand comes from. Services are, as the name suggests, consulting services that are provided. Sectors are the industry segments that buy these services, like mining, pharmaceutical, defense, retail, manufacturing, oil and gas, telecommunications etc.

Creating cells that provide a service, which in turn is in demand within one sector, and further has the opportunity to be introduced to other sectors, should be your primary aim in a growth model. Step one is creating the first one or two cells to meet your initial client niche demand. Step two is not necessarily creating more cells, it is also the discipline of cross-marketing.

A services-and-sectors model is quite powerful in achieving cross-marketing. Let's look at cross-marketing on a larger scale, and then it will be simple to apply it to your smaller scale business. The cross-marketing approach does two things. First, it sells multiple services into a single client sector. If your brand name is well respected by, say, the banking industry, you attempt to create more revenue from that industry by supplying other services to it, essentially leveraging off your reputation and goodwill. Often, your service level is key to selling multiple services in a client organization or a client sector. If the experience of how you do the thing that you do is well regarded (your service level), cross marketing within a sector becomes easier. Why? Because the people in one client sector network with each other far more than people across multiple sectors do. And if you're well-regarded by one or two clients in, for example, telecommunications company A, word of mouth will allow you to convert that goodwill to an entrée into telecommunications company B.

Second, the cross marketing approach builds excellence in a service offering, and uses this excellence to break into new sectors in which the service carries value. So you become known for excellence in a service that had applications in several sectors, and this excellence becomes your entrée to other sectors. In my experience this is much harder to do unless you have genuine innovation that is in demand across other sectors.

So the very loose rule of thumb is that good service provides cross marketing within the same sector, and excellence and innovation allows you to introduce new sectors into your client portfolio. It is a loose rule because it's not hard to show exceptions, but if you are looking for an underlying pattern of growth, it's useful to recognize these two cross-marketing tools.

When you are building your own consulting firm, you start with – typically – one service and a couple of sectors. For example, you might consult in change management systems for retail industries and manufacturing. Or you might consult in environmental controls for oil companies and mining companies.

A useful approach to growth is to understand two or three sectors intimately. I reason that if I can understand a couple of sectors well, I might gain some insights into the most useful collection of services around which I could build Small-Niche-Bands. Which sectors you pick will really depend on how ambitious you are.

For example, you ambition might be to become international, if not global. Here I mean 'real' international, as opposed to an "Ireland is international to England" approach. This narrows down your sector options to industries that have traditionally operated in several parts of the world, linked by a global market for the commodity or service that they deliver. An example of one such industry is oil and gas; an example of an industry that would *not* fit that mold well is the dairy industry.

### The U in fun

*It's worth pointing out here that when it comes to strategy, bigger is not necessarily better, nor more profitable, nor more exit-strategy-friendly. In my case, the choice to be genuinely international was driven by ego, not by financial acumen. Had we been more financially driven, we would have selected low entry-cost national sectors with national growth potential. Our drivers, instead, were to work on exciting international projects in unique parts of the world. Travel and a jet-setting lifestyle were (and I say this shamelessly while acknowledging that it sounds commercially naïve and somewhat shallow) a driver, not a result of decisions we made. Every year, during the first few years, I ran some what-if analyses to understand better how much value we were giving away by indulging a James Bond fantasy.*

*We were definitely giving away value. But the un-quantified upside was that it was giving me a tremendous amount of job satisfaction. In my mid to late thirties, I was an owner of a thriving and rapidly growing boutique consulting business working at Board and Executive levels for several Fortune 500 companies. We were called in to troubleshoot projects in exotic locations all over the world. Our staff members were working on projects that they would not have imagined working on, in their previous lives. Sometimes they were even leading these projects.*

*I worked hard, but most of the time it didn't feel like work. It felt like high-jinks fun. This is part of the formula for success. It has to feel like an adventure, not like a slog. Climbing Everest is hard work (I've never done it but I assume it's not a trivial exercise) but it's also a tremendous adventure. It was important to me that the consulting business I was leading gave me satisfaction, and the source of that satisfaction lay in the things that I found personally fulfilling. The work – the thing I was good at – was an integral part of that fulfillment, but it was by no means the only aspect of self-fulfillment. At some point, as I approached my Exit Strategy, it wasn't even the main part of my own personal fulfillment.*

## The power of resilience

When you're striving for "more yes than no" in your strategy, your ability to handle the "no" moments is critical. They will happen, and they will test your resilience.

This resilience is important, because in a small company you are the focal point. You're the satellite dish that transmits, through word and deed (as well as the absence or insufficient amount of either) the governing 'vibe' of the organization. The vibe you project is amplified, quite alarmingly, through the words and actions of the majority of your staff. Something you might think innocuous can get beamed back at you, weeks or months later, at many times the wattage. If you project despair, you'll reap despair. If you project enthusiasm, you'll see lots of it back from your staff. Small enterprises have an uncanny ability to mold themselves in your image.

## Being more right than wrong

In my first enterprise, our selection of Small-Niche-Band skills – the building blocks of our company – was not pre-planned all the way to the Exit Strategy, and to the actual Exit. Once we selected sectors that we knew reasonably well (it's important to start with your strengths) and which supported our broad vision, we set about becoming as knowledgeable about them as we could. I selected three sectors to focus on. We ensured we understood their value chains, their general market economics, and the supply-and-demand mechanics of the commodities they delivered. We understood how they were structured – or more precisely, the range of conventional and unconventional management structures that these industries adopted. We understood their challenges in the present, and we had a fair notion of their future challenges, thus making us both operationally and strategically relevant to these industries. In truth, this chapter could go on for a very long time, because the insights mined from understanding sectors seemed to come from an inexhaustible supply. But chief among these insights was a short list of services that we could provide today, a much longer list of the linked services we could provide over time, and a roadmap for sequencing how we might grow our service offerings from today's list to tomorrow's list.

The lists (both today's and tomorrow's) were not static. They changed, and were reviewed dogmatically every six months. Today's list changed as we grew, and it changed through accretion, not through substitution. We added service offerings, and the care we applied in adding them paid off as we never actually had to remove them from our portfolio even though their fortunes waxed and waned in echoed tune to the boom-and-bust industrial cycles. Every service offering we added remained relevant and added value to our company. Some would be cash cows for longer than others, some were mediocre for longer than others, *but none actually became redundant. For a while I thought we were just lucky, but hindsight tells me we chose our services carefully and well.*

*Tomorrow's long list didn't change much, but the sequencing we applied did change quite a bit. Services that seemed like a good bet just a year ago would be superseded by others that seemed like a better strategic fit. Economic cycles are dynamic, and so sectors of companies that seem bankable in one decade may appear less attractive in the next. Some growth areas might have a sustained meteoric upswing, but most mature industries ebb and flow with world economic conditions. Not every choice we made was flawless, but the individual and cumulative wisdom of those choices eventually consolidated into our "more yes than no" bundle.*

## Seeking cycles

The analysis of cycles works. It isn't a mathematically precise analysis, but it is supported by macro scale data. If the time between the inception of your enterprise and the all-important Exit is a few years, then picking upswing sector winners is potentially a good strategy. Of course, the Global Financial Crisis (the GFC) of 2008 was a rule-breaker as it somewhat indiscriminately tore through a wide variety of sectors in a stunning domino effect. It wasn't part of a cyclic event, at least not in the way we had thought of cycles. It was a whole new mechanism of failure. Our conventional wisdom would not have prepared us for the GFC.

Post-GFC though, whilst there are regional tremors and warnings of future disruptions, cyclic economic processes seem to continue. With 'sustainable' commodities, this makes sense. Supply-and-demand is a tango, with supply swinging over demand, then the pendulum reversing to correct, and overcorrection a constant beat of the tune.

Those are the mechanics of picking what you do. The science behind your choices of sectors and services helps you identify and sequence your growth path. Equally important, if not more so, is that your choices energize you. Remember, you are growing a company. Your employees feed off your energy. So choose carefully from that list the things you, as a professional, genuinely want to do. Choose things that will keep you, the owner, enthusiastic and vibrant.

Of course, it's highly unlikely that the sector that's on an upward trend, the service that's emerging or sustainable and has more demand than supply, *and* the thing that floats your boat personally are – hey presto – also the most profitable thing to do. That would be a minor miracle. And so you have choices to make. I've never just invested in the most profitable services and sectors; I've invested in an integrated portfolio that balances success with fun.

Naturally, you'll never know if the choices you did not make could have made you more successful. You'll only know if the choices you make *were* successful in their own right, and whether they kept you energized. You may make choices that are less profitable in the short term, but you may believe they propagate your growth better.

March to your own tune, not everyone else's. In a competitive world, the most attractive propositions will be the sectors and – particularly – the services that are the most profitable. The most attractive propositions, by their definition, attract the most competitors. In that scenario – in most cases at least – supply soon exceeds demand, fuelled by a "gold rush" dynamic. Those services have a long-run deterioration in profitability if there is an element of price-competitiveness in the market. In other words, if there are too many of you offering the same service, prices go down, margins get squeezed and everyone loses something. In very few cases, where clients buy high-end quality with a lesser regard for price, it is possible to stay above the rabble. But your strategy, to borrow from a basketball metaphor, should be based on high-percentage two-pointer shots, not low-percentage three-pointers.

There is a subtlety here. I am not suggesting that you ignore obvious high-profit services. Quite the opposite in fact. There is nothing wrong, and many things right, with being an active part of "gold rush" propositions. Just don't pivot your growth strategy on them. Use them to provide cash flow to grow the things you really want to grow.

I have always deliberately chosen services that I, as an individual, had a passion for, and I accepted that they might be less profitable in the short term. I focused on turning these services into signature offerings by investing senior time in developing a high level of consistent quality in the way we provided the services. In my experience, these "signature services" were almost never the cash cows that most consultants chased with feverish excitement, but they were quietly, confidently and sustainably valuable to the sectors I operated in.

These choices fuelled growth for two reasons. One was that they were bankable services for the sectors I wanted to work in. Some were new and emerging, but with significant prospects for a five to ten-year outlook. The other reason was that the choices fuelled my own individual enthusiasm, which in turn infected most of the staff. The first reason gave me a stable proposition; something I would enjoy. The second reason was integral to what a management consultant I engaged once referred to as a "kick-ass culture of growth".

### Recognizing invisible strengths

*In one of the firms I started, we had proved our formula surprisingly early in our evolution, and applied it relentlessly afterward. We had developed a small but useful reputation for excellence in an emerging field of consulting, for a few mining, oil and gas companies. Not many of our consulting competitors had chosen to enter the same market because its research investment cost was high. There wasn't yet a cookie-cutter approach to the service that would increase margins to highly attractive levels.*

*The CEO of an industry group mentioned our expertise to a wildly successful oil company, and they in turn invited us to pitch our service to them. The problem was that they had also asked two of the Big Four global management consulting groups to pitch to them. We thought about it long and hard, and we had misgivings. Sending a team to pitch to the overseas-based company was expensive, and the competitors were household names. We were virtually unknown.*

*I was enthusiastic, but I baulked at the expense of sending a whole team. In the end, I went alone, well-prepared by my home team. The client offices were kitted with oak paneling, dim lighting and the residual aroma of cigar smoke. The two Big Four companies pitched before I did; two teams of four slickly-dressed professionals, two hours each. By the time it was my turn to enter the Boardroom, I was consoling myself that it had been worth a shot, and perhaps I'd have a mini-break and do some sightseeing on the way back home.*

*I pitched to a group of somber people in the Boardroom, did my best, and on the way out planned my consolation sightseeing weekend. But astonishingly, I was called up to their offices before I left, and told by one of the Board members we had won the contract. Before I could stop myself,*

*I asked why. I must have looked startled; I certainly felt it. The answer I received validated our budding theory. It turns out we had a genuine depth of insight in the area. We had a unique and well-developed way of thinking. We came across as a group that was excellent at this work, not a group who did this work to supplement revenue. And, although this was indeed our strategy, we had worked so hard at it, so close to the wheel, that we had forgotten it was our strength.*

*For us, it was a giant-killing validation that a David with a well-tuned slingshot could neutralize a couple of Goliaths. We retained the contract every year, without competition, until the company was sold. It turned out to be one of our most lucrative contracts, it embellished our fame in the area and it led to other similar successes for that service.*

## The power of self-belief

In a very short time, the greatest source of pride for our staff was that, in the areas we chose to be good at, we were very successful. The formula allowed us to be competitive in environments that other minnow consulting firms would avoid. Our staff became fearless and confident, and understood that being labeled a boutique consulting firm did not just mean you were small. It meant you were choosy, quality, even elite. The Managing Directors of seasoned consulting firms were, according to some of our clients, nervous when we were invited to submit proposals for work that they were considering competing for. It was a source of amusement to our clients, perhaps the subversive anticipation of seeing the Christian kill the lion for a change. We acquired a wildcard status quickly, and we enjoyed this status. As an owner, it kept me fresh and enthusiastic. Work was not so much about revenue and profit as it was about being potent in the consulting world. Revenues and profits were, to us, a natural byproduct of being potent. And that's why, for me at least, work was an adventure.

## THREE TIPS

*Tip one*: Focus on making the adventure fun. The hard work will not matter, provided it is fun.

*Tip two*: Structuring your organization around sectors and services allows you to be more specific about your presence in the market, and it allows you to keep a perspective on what's fun and exciting.

*Tip three*: A strategy formed around 'cells' allows you to build nimbleness and resilience in your organization, and – like blocks of Lego – it makes the building of your enterprise easier.

# CHAPTER 6
# GROW WITH PURPOSE

*Do, or do not. There is no try*
*- Yoda*

## The mechanics of growth

Growing. Every living thing does it without trying. For most living organisms it just happens. We don't think about it. There is no strategy involved in growing. There is a chemical and biological sequence that occurs, and your son, daughter, nephew or niece adds another inch to his or her height.

When I started my first consulting firm, I was looking for the sequence that – as closely as possible – automated growth. Or, more precisely, told you when to grow. I had been consulting for a large company for a few years, and I realized that growth strategies were part art, part science.

While I appreciated and respected the talent a manager requires to harness both art and science, I personally wanted as little as possible of the art in my methodology. It allowed for too many interpretations of signals for growth. At its worst, it allowed 'forced growth' to occur, resulting in growth spurts that were reversed within months, leading to wasted resources in achieving the growth, and evaporated profits in dealing with the pain of downsizing. At its most mediocre, it led to contract labor practices, increasing the unit cost of labor while harnessing temporary growth, creating an illusion of growth and prosperity.

I also had watched managers grow their consulting units or offices for many reasons. Some were purely egotistical, empire-building reasons. Others, driven by a Key Performance Indicator from their own manager, or a head office mandate, developed poor foundations for growth, achieving short term growth (and hence their short-term bonus) in one year.

With these poor foundations, the growth could be reversed the next year and no short term bonus gained. But a bonus in one year followed by no bonus the next year is better than no bonus at all over two years, so there was no disincentive for this unsustainable practice. Of course, there were examples of sustained growth, but I was appalled that for every such example I could point to several other abject failures.

## Profit versus growth

To manage any enterprise, understanding the finances is crucial. From capital spending to cashflow, managing monetary matters ranks as one of the top skills required by managers and leaders. Unfortunately, not all of us are trained in finance. If you have a valuable consulting skill, and it's not based on capital spending and cashflow, where does that leave you when you are trying to grow an office, or to grow a service in a consulting firm?

I spent a few years watching managers in large companies deal with this skills mismatch. It was a revealing experience. I realized that a layman's view of a profit and loss statement was a dangerously limiting thing. Everyone understands that Profit is Revenue minus Expenditure. There is nothing magical in that equation. It costs me $1.50 to make a hot dog and I sell it for $2.50. My profit is $1.

In consulting, because you are creating value with human resources and supporting expenditure, expenditure is largely within your control. To make my hot dog on the other hand, I rely on market costs of the bread roll, the sausage, the mustard and the ketchup. Although I can make choices about where and how I buy these things, I am in a supply chain and there is only so much I can do about the things that happen before we get to my link of the chain. I certainly can't influence the price of sausages, or the cost of the bottle of mustard. So if I'm asked to increase my profit by 20 cents, there is only so much give in the expenditure line. If I want to increase my profit by 20 cents, I'll charge $2.70.

Contrast this with consulting. It is not within a classic supply chain. Most of your value resides in peoples' heads. You have a set of overheads that you support to keep people happy, creative and productive in extracting the value from their brains. Office space, desks, computers, air conditioning, biscuits, coffee, marketing budgets, décor and many others are part of the set of overheads you provide.

If I ask a consulting manager to increase profits by five percent (with a bonus incentive of course), the *very easiest* thing to do is to reduce expenditure because my supply chain is very short. Of course, the manager will have a go at increasing revenue. But it's uncertain whether he or she will attain revenue goals. To be more confident of achieving profit margins, it's easier to tackle the known quantities. Look at the expenditure list, and seek ways of reducing it. Obvious questions arise. Why do we need so much office space? Why are the bonuses for junior people so generous? Business class and first class flights… why? And why on earth do we need chocolate biscuits?

In most cases, it's perfectly possible to Scrooge your way into a higher profit margin. This is not automatically a bad thing, because frivolous expenditure will harm any enterprise, and a little bit of Scrooge in manageable doses is healthy. But if it becomes a runaway method of management, it risks achieving the reverse of what you'd hope for. It risks lower productivity, lower creativity, greater turnover and – let's face it – it risks creating a place that is not fun to work in.

Consulting managers are generally not blessed with creative business and financial management skills. Lawyers, engineers, graphic designers, advertising consultants and even economists are not taught that expenditure reduction is a limited strategy. You can only do so much before the floor hits the basement. The roof, on the other hand, can keep extending to the sky. These are not insights they teach at engineering school or law school.

As a younger consultant, I had excellent consulting mentors, some of whom had IQs of Einsteinian proportions. But this was often their Achilles' heel, this one-dimensional ability to navigate a profit and loss equation. Incredibly talented consulting managers could simply not create sustainable growth. They could talk the hind leg off a donkey, sell ice to Eskimos, and find solutions to problems that you would not have believed existed. But they could not do what their ten-year old child did every day – grow continuously, relentlessly.

This didn't mean they were failures. There are other ways to create growth. Fund it.

You could, for example, buy a successful business and assimilate it into your arsenal. This is a bit like growing by grafting a third arm onto your armpit. You *do* grow. Your weight increases by a few percent. You get more done because, as we all know, many hands make light work.

You could find some money to invest in a new sector or new service, nurture it and grow it. This is quite sensible provided you can find some money. Sometimes, this is a big *if*. When it's just you and perhaps a few people in your consulting firm, bankrolling investments can be a challenge.

### Exponential returns

*When I developed my first consulting firm, there was just a modest amount of cash. The house was re-mortgaged to allow for this.*

*I had a deep aversion towards debt. Now, a pathological dislike of debt is not financially astute; but there you go, that's what I had in my psychological makeup. As I pointed out before, consultants are typically not bred with any kind of keen financial insights.*

*Some years later, after this first consulting company was sold, I calculated the return on investment on that modest mortgage extension at about two hundred and twenty percent per year, compounding. This was, admittedly, off a small investment, which isn't going to affect world economics, although it was clearly a very efficient way to increase wealth. Equally noteworthy is that the return on investment occurred without incurring debt in the company, or incurring further personal debt. In other words, there was no further leverage.*

*I didn't realize how remarkable the average compounding rate of return on the investment was, until I had sold the firm and was figuring out what to do next. I was discussing, with a number of potential investors, a copper mining prospect that we were considering, for which*

*I was invited to sit on the Board. One of the investors was a seventy-five year old High Net Worth Individual, a former football star from the 1960s who had turned entrepreneur and had created and sold successful businesses for most of his life. I was awed by his track record of brilliant investments, and sheepishly kept any details of my one modest success to myself. We were discussing the return on investment of the potential copper mine over several years, and considering floating the entity on the stock exchange. Naturally, this would result in a very healthy return on investment for all of us, but somewhat short of the two hundred and twenty percent per year I had experienced before. We were poring over financial projections and discussing options over lunch. I mused out loud that we should work through the concept more and see if we could hit an average rate of return of a hundred and fifty or two hundred percent per year.*

*The High Net Worth Individual looked at me, startled.*

*"We'd need to find high grade gold in there as well, if we're to consider anything like that kind of return," he replied gruffly.*

*I suddenly doubted if I had gotten my calculation right for my own first consulting investment, years before. When I went home that weekend, I dug out the financial records from that consulting enterprise and recalculated the return on investment. It didn't change; I hadn't made a mistake. There must have been some high grade gold in our approach back then.*

## Growing without growing pains

There are three ingredients I always try to bake into a consulting business, and I advise others of the same. I believe that if you achieve all three, it's almost impossible to avoid success. One is a more 'automated' decision making process for growth, particularly answering the "when to grow" question. Two is that managers apply a profit focus that does not default to the control of expenditure as their main game. Three is self-funded growth; in other words, if you can manage it, don't borrow to create growth. I'm aware the last is not conventional wisdom; it's a personal preference. However, after the Global Financial Crisis, it probably does qualify as some kind of wisdom.

When I started my first entrepreneurial venture, I had a theoretical answer to the "how to" question that gave me all three desirable outcomes, but I had never put it into practice. While doing my MBA, I had done my thesis on the development of a global consulting business. The thesis looked at international growth and business roll-out models in Asia, and wasn't overly technical. But while thinking through the practicalities of developing businesses, I developed a theoretical model for growth that addressed the three ingredients I wanted to apply to consulting businesses.

When I started my first consulting firm, I dusted this model off, and it formed the basis of the red-wine/Spiderman lecture in Chapter two that I delivered to my two colleagues.

The theory works this way. Obviously, the relationship that Profit equals Revenue minus Expenditure is simple, and everyone gets it. But it's too simple, and it would be seductively easy for people to focus overly on expenditure as a 'cheap' way to maximize profit. So the theory begins by breaking every rule regarding Keeping It Simple, and complicates the humble profit equation.

Let's make a set of very straightforward assumptions. One was that you are paying people to use their brains, therefore your prime asset is people and their prime cost is their salaries. You use their salaries to earn fees, so your key lever is the ratio of fees to salaries. The higher the ratio of fees to salaries, the better the leverage. If fees are $f$ and salaries are $s$, the following ratio is very important to you,

$$\frac{f}{s}$$

The other straightforward assumption is that you need to control costs, but that the costs are simply supporting your people. Your total costs, $tc$, are the sum of your salary costs, $s$, and the supporting costs – call them overheads – $c$. In other words,

$$tc = s + c$$

Your lever on costs can be expressed as

$$\frac{s}{tc}$$

You don't want this to get too small, in other words don't allow your overhead costs to dominate and therefore make the denominator too large. The cost lever can only be as high as 1.0, which is when you have no supporting costs and you put Scrooge to shame.

These two ratios, $f/s$ and $s/tc$, became my two driving performance indicators. But what are good ratios, as opposed to average or poor ratios? How do they relate to profits and profitability?

The humble profit equation is

$$Profit = Revenue - Expenditure$$

…which in our language is fees less total costs, or

$$Profit = f - tc$$

Profitability, which is your percentage profit, is your profit divided by your revenue (or the proportion of your revenue – your fees – that settles comfortably in the bank).

$$\frac{Profit}{f} = 1 - \frac{tc}{f}$$

which is the same as saying

$$Profitability = 1 - \frac{tc}{f}$$

which, by some simple algebra, is identical to

$$Profitability = 1 - \frac{1}{\left(\frac{f}{s}\right)\left(\frac{s}{tc}\right)}$$

For those readers unfamiliar with, afraid of, or simply irritated by algebra, I apologize for this nerdy departure into high school mathematics. However, I urge you to try and understand it, because it will unlock incredible financial potential in your consulting company.

I have explained this theory to every one of my employees in a number of consulting firms over the period of more than a decade. The reality, of course, is that understanding the theory is completely irrelevant to the ability to practice it. You don't need to understand the workings of an internal combustion engine or a hybrid engine to actually drive a car. But I've always believed that every one of my employees should understand that all I had done was find two useful levers to make the humble profit equation operationally relevant and growth-oriented – in other words, there was no new business theory here.

Despite my efforts over many years to explain the theory, I can probably guarantee that not one single employee from my past or present consulting enterprises will remember it, because most people don't like equations.

Now let's look at how this translates to profitability, then we'll identify the "zone of success", and then I'll explain how the limiting behaviors of consulting managers discussed at the start of this chapter were mostly overcome by this model of business management.

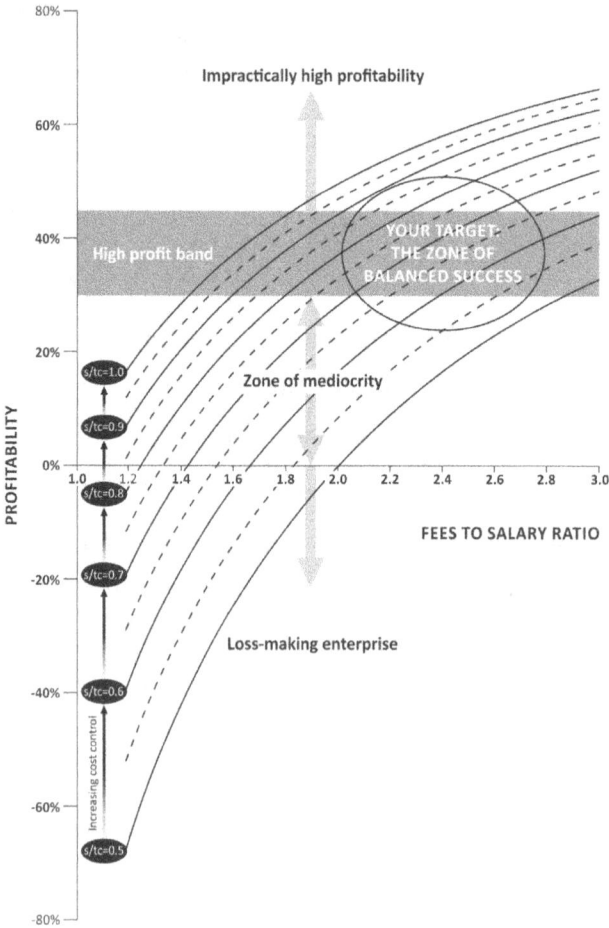

The figure contains a wealth of information, and it is worth examining closely. It shows the translation to profitability and identifies the zone of success. The horizontal axis is the fees to salary ratio, plotted from 1.0 to 3.0. The vertical axis is profitability, plotted from minus 80% (a disaster) to plus 80% (which is so improbably high that it sounds illegal).

The series of curves plots the profitability against fees to salary ratios, for a range of salary to total cost ratios. The salary to total cost ratios plotted vary from 0.5 (extremely high overheads) to 1.0 (impossibly tight, no overheads, and a cost-management effort Scrooge would be proud of).

These were the two financial key performance indicators for our consulting cells and our offices. The fees to salary ratio was the driving force. If we were riding a bicycle, they were the pedals. The salary to total cost ratio was much easier to manage and only needed fine adjustments most of the time, like the handlebars of a bicycle.

From the graph, it is then a matter of picking your target. Let's say your salary to total cost ratio sits at around 0.7. At a fees to salary ratio of 2.2, profitability is around 35 percent. This is not hard to do if your managers' operating behaviors are right. And most business owners salivate over profits like that.

### The automatic engine

*Most small companies make 10 to 15 percent profit. I had worked in large construction firms who refused to bid for projects under $400 million, and their profits were 12 percent on a good year. Legal and accounting firms were a lot more lucrative, and a profitability in the low twenties was not uncommon. The consulting firm I had worked in had once made 17 percent in a year, and the celebrations had been orgasmic.*

*By Year Three of my first consulting effort, we had grown phenomenally, and had two national offices and two international offices. Our profitability was high and we were a significant threat to our competitors; both for their clients and for their staff. I recall our financial manager walking into my office one afternoon, a quizzical expression on her face and two magazines in her hand. One was Forbes magazine, and the other was a national business magazine lift-out that was published one day in each month in a national newspaper.*

*"We should be in this list," she said earnestly, but still with that quizzical expression on her face. I asked what list she was thinking of. She opened the Forbes magazine, which had an article on the most profitable businesses of the last few years, and the business magazine, which had the country's "Hot 100" growth businesses, and profiles of their owners.*

*She was right. Forbes listed Tier One companies – the most profitable companies – at an average profitability of 16.5 percent. The top five or six of the Hot 100 had year-on-year growth rates (growth in revenues) of fifty percent or more over three year averages. Our profitability was about twice the average of that of Forbes' Tier One firms, and we were easily in the revenue growth rate bracket of the top five or six in the country.*

*She was quizzical because it didn't seem right. And it's true, it felt surreal. But the numbers didn't lie. I pointed out that we did, to be fair, distribute a lot of that profit, and we used much of the profit to start up new businesses and grow. So Gross Profit wasn't the best measure, and perhaps we weren't really comparing apples with apples in this case. Still, it was a flattering realization that our performance put us in the company of some enviably successful businesses.*

*It would have been fun to enter ourselves in these prestigious lists, but I decided to keep a low profile. We were still a very long way off the*

*Exit Strategy, and I didn't particularly want suitors distracting us from our work with offers of a buyout.*

## Managing growth

Translating this model to growth is reasonably straightforward. If you have a mandate to grow, every manager of every cell should be focused on that mandate. A simple automatic rule might be that if a cell meets a fees to salary ratio of 2.3 or above for three months in a row, it should grow. The actual number (typically in the range 2.0 to 2.6) is calculated based on your Exit Strategy. If you are less aggressive in growth and more profit focused, you might choose a fees to salary ratio of 2.5 or more. Track fees to salary ratios weekly, and if a cell's prognosis for the second or third month in a row is looking good, you might initiate a growth conversation.

The above is just an example, and one that worked well for me. Any consulting business can define its own metrics using fees-to-salary and salary-to-total cost. The trick is not so much to set the goals, it is to manage them.

At this point, it is important that I confess that automatic growth is a bit of a misnomer. Not every growth conversation results in an automatic decision to grow. It is important to consider whether growth is sustainable, and not just growth for the sake of growth. Be judicious about choices to grow. What the process does is to focus each of your managers on profitability through fees and the growth model, rather than the cost control model of low growth profitability. It means that you can continually – and by continually I do mean every month – address one or more growth prospects.

When you grow multiple offices, the balance of the fees-to-salary model becomes more of an art form. Think of playing an instrument, and then think of conducting a small orchestra. The pace of growth is different for each office – in other words each instrument has a different part to play – but the overriding model applies for the whole organisation. So your whole orchestra is geared to a fees-to-salary ratio of say 2.2, but individual offices may run at 2.5, or 2.1, or 2.0.

A word of caution – I have found this orchestration needs a lot of concentration if you want to manage it well. In one company that used this model, as we grew internationally, the pace of growth became frenetic, and complicated by foreign exchange considerations, tax implications and sovereign risk issues. Think of those instruments, playing not in a controlled amphitheatre, but on a gusty beach where sound travels and dissipates.

The cell model, the fees to salary model of profitability and the growth mandate at fees to salaries of [insert your number here!] means that you can have multiple drivers of growth and profit throughout the business. Managers and general managers don't need to look at profit and loss accounts at any other time than the end of a financial year. Their key performance indicators are clear and simple, and focused on profitability and growth. Under those conditions, running a business is noticeably simplified, and it makes time in your schedule as an owner to focus on the people aspects of your business, where the real value lies.

## THREE TIPS

*Tip one*: The profit-and-loss account, that stalwart of accountants everywhere, is useful and necessary for your tax requirements, if nothing else. It may not be the best dashboard for your managers. Remember that the people you hire – the talented consultants – are often not natural-born (or adequately trained) business managers or business growth specialists. Break with convention and give them simple management and growth models to work with.

*Tip two*: Don't listen to the naysayers. High-profit, high-growth is perfectly feasible if you think in cells, growth thresholds and topline revenues. Don't settle for low-profit, high-growth; or high-profit, low growth. That's what everyone else does.

*Tip three*: Keep your discipline. You might incentivize your entire organization, to grow, but pick where you grow and when. Grow when you are ready to grow, and grow in cells.

# CHAPTER 7
# DEBT-FREE GROWTH

*Money often costs too much*
*– Ralph Waldo Emerson*

## The case against borrowing money

In the last chapter, we concluded that balancing profitability and growth is an art. You have to pay close attention to the present and the near future, predict the things that may change in each, and act accordingly.

Being profitable and growing, without falling into debt, is an even tougher proposition. Before pursuing this subject, I should point out that it is not at all unwise to borrow money to grow. There is a reason that banks have been around for a long time. Borrowing money to grow works, it has been a successful practice for hundreds of years, and it is beneficial for both lender and borrower. If you want to own your own home, you are likely to start off by going into debt. And it can be mind-numbing, future-limiting debt. But it is often a necessary evil. And while many people might manage to coexist with it, I believe that you, me, and every other entrepreneur are at our happiest without debt, thank you very much.

If you're not already sold on it, here are four reasons for growing a successful business without borrowing. One is that you are focusing on growing a small non-capital-intensive business, and such small businesses are not particularly hungry for cash. Two is that owing anyone money – the burden of debt – is something most people genuinely dislike. Three is that the more you owe, the less control you have of your own destiny (although admittedly you can negotiate around this one in lending agreements). And four is – quite simply – because you can.

Now, I don't believe you can grow perpetually without cash injections into your business. So if you are determined to grow without borrowing, you should reconcile yourself with the likelihood that there is only so much growth you will be able to achieve, or there will come a time when your rate of growth can no longer increase. If you carefully plot the path to your Exit Strategy by analysing growth and cashflow, you will find out what that horizon looks like for you.

Doing your arithmetic correctly and comprehensively before the start of your enterprise journey is important. Obviously, unless you're channelling a particularly accurate Nostradamus, your predictions will, more likely than not, be incorrect. What's more important is that you understand your assumptions and what they mean to your business growth and its financing, and that you are ready to re-forecast your plan if one or more of your assumptions proves to be wrong. It's a little-acknowledged but powerful part of the discipline of entrepreneurs. Plan it in excruciating detail, then expect it all to change.

### The pain of credit

When I first started my first consulting firm, I extended my already significant mortgage on the family home. The extension took me to the maximum borrowable sum for the home, and it was only a modest amount with which to start a consulting firm. I was up to my eyebrows in debt. We had just had our third child; arguably not the best timing to take a risk, quit my job and start my own enterprise. For the first two months, while revenue in the company was slowly warming up, I could only afford to pay myself a small salary – a fraction of what I was getting before in a full time job. Most of that money went towards servicing the mortgage, and my credit cards were getting overloaded as I struggled to maintain the family lifestyle by progressively extending the debt on those cards. I was in the local supermarket, my wife herding our two older children and carrying our youngest while I wheeled the trolley to the checkout. Appallingly, my credit card was declined. I tried my backup credit card, which was also declined. Embarrassed and stealing furtive glances at the impatient customers in the line behind us, I took some items out of the shopping trolley and asked the cashier to try again. This time the credit card transaction went through. Mortified at the fuss that had been caused, we skulked away from the supermarket.

And that, in a nutshell, was what bothered me about credit. Someone else – not me – held the financial decision-making in the palm of his or her hands. That was not the type of enterprise I wanted to own and lead. I wanted complete, unadulterated, unquestioned independence to make my own decisions.

## Cash is king

Achieving self-funded growth is a deeply satisfying experience but it is very taxing, no pun intended. Avoiding the spectre of debt while running a growing business soon becomes an experience that is not unlike juggling.

In the last chapter I expanded on the growth model, and it is necessary to qualify a few things now in order to clarify how we maintained debt-free growth.

The fees to salary model usually delivers multiple growth options. Suppose you have ten consulting cells running, and four are operating at fees to salary ratios of 2.3 and above for three or more months in a row (your Key Performance Indicator relating to growth, as an example). You don't need (or necessarily want) to grow in all four cells simultaneously. You could pick one, or two, at the most. There are a number of factors that should be considered before picking these, including the nature of the service, its existing and future demand by clients, the breadth of clients presenting with this demand, the attractiveness of other services you could start (i.e., an eleventh cell rather than an investment in one of the existing ten cells), the availability in the market of consultants, how much it would cost to grow and, of course, how much you can afford. The affordability criterion should be dictated, in true cash-is-king form, by how much banked profit has accumulated during the three months prior, by all of the cells in operation. There is no need to spend more than you have in the bank.

What happens when you grow – and this is especially true in consulting firms whose main expenditure is salaries – is that the cost of employment builds rapidly to frighteningly high levels. Because wages are paid at a set time (for example, monthly), each month has a looming and very large expenditure that has absolutely no flexibility in timing. You simply have to make, on time, your salary costs as well as other costs related to personnel, such as taxes and superannuation.

Clients, however, are not faced with the same extreme sensitivity to timing when they pay your bills. In fact, there is often a despairing level of ambivalence by clients to paying bills on time. Work done in Month One will, if you are lucky, be paid for in Month Two (or more likely in Month Three or even Month Four), and some clients had no difficulty in extending this to Month Six. Interestingly, I have found that the big client companies were equally, if not more likely, to pay late than smaller client companies. So much for their flashy SAP systems!

If anything is going to derail your self-funding growth plans, this aspect is a strong candidate. In my first consulting foray, I had (wisely, I thought) anticipated this trend, but had completely underestimated the size of its effect. As the enterprises grow larger, you fall further and further to the mercy of clients who pay late. Where once your bailout funds might cover you for some late payments, eventually the size of the bailout fund looks like a small country's GDP. You sleep less and less soundly at night. You get frustrated with your clients. The compulsion to go into debt to create your buffer becomes almost too much to ignore. How can you get your clients to support your cashflow, not create a cashflow crisis?

## Understanding your debtors

It's very important to develop some kind of custodianship of the revenue loop that runs between your invoicing and your accounts receivable. The first, and most important, part of the custodianship is your relationship with the client. It must be strong enough and warm enough to address, without recrimination, potentially late payments. This should be important enough to you that you take a personal stake in client payment timings, at least in the early stages of your enterprise.

The second part of the custodianship is setting the contract arrangements in a way that supports payments on time. The reason this is done is that very often your client contact, the person who made the decision to hire you, has no special relationship with his or her accounting section. So you might lean on him or her to pay on time, but all his or her leaning on the client's accounting section amounts to nothing. Unless he or she can point to a contract clause that mandates the payment in a specified time. A clause that – ideally – has a compelling disincentive for late payment practices, such as ceasing work (a very confronting clause to include in a contract) or a financial penalty (more palatable, but still somewhat a touchy subject).

The third part is understanding your client's accounting processes. Many late payments are triggered by invoices that raise some kind of accounting, administrative or contractual question – some ambiguity, missing information, incorrect cost codings or other data. Your invoice goes from the top of the pile in the "in" tray to the "issues pending" tray that hopefully will receive some attention when the "in" tray is empty. And if your client is a large organisation, their "in" tray is a perpetually growing beast. You definitely do not want your invoice to lose its place in that tray.

Understanding how to craft your invoices so that each client finds it easy to pay is, literally, gold. Unfortunately, every client has a different set of requirements to achieve this ease. Being flexible enough to make your invoicing bespoke for your clients, or at least the ones receiving big bills, is an advantage. It sounds like extra work, doesn't it? It is. It sounds inefficient, and I won't argue with you on that point.

But, inefficient as it is, it is more *effective* to think this way than to nurture some kind of misguided administrative ego that tells you – with a petulant stamp of its foot – that people should pay on time when they receive a bill. It's your business, and cashflow is the lifeblood of your business. Don't risk clogged arteries.

The discipline of shepherding invoices is one of the most powerful disciplines to get right if you want a self-funding growth firm. The other is cashflow smoothing.

Cashflow smoothing is difficult to achieve. A significant part of cashflow smoothing is avoiding pinch points in your cash cycle. The end-of-month wages are a pinch point. The flood of revenue from the invoices sent out last month is also another pinch point. Quite bizarrely, most businesses pay wages and do all their invoices at the end of the month. This means that at the end of each month, you are doing two things simultaneously. You are paying a massive bill, and you are sending out requests for revenue. If you think about it logically, that is a painful way to live.

Staggered billing is a useful way to "smear" your revenue stream so that it is more steady. It doesn't solve the problem of course, but it does ease it, and its psychologically quite calming to see a steady flow of revenue rather than sudden bursts of cash through the door. Even though the sudden bursts of cash might dizzyingly feel like you've won the lottery, I can promise you that your heart can only take so much lottery-winning. It's simply no fun to be holding your breath waiting for lumps of revenue to come in. Take away the lumpiness, and you will live longer.

### *Show me the money*

*I used to work for a consultant who, like me (but many years earlier) had started his own consulting firm and then sold it to a large multi-national. While not quite a mentor, he was always generous with his advice. One of his recommendations, when I started my own firm with a business partner, was to manage the finances closely. "Cash is king," he said. "Make sure you know where your cash is coming from and going to, every day. If you don't, then you're flirting with bankruptcy."*

*Personally, at the time, I thought that was one of the most boringly administrative pieces of advice I had ever heard. I was used to more visionary advice, and this just sounded like an accountant's Monday-morning monologue. It turned out to be the most important piece of business advice I have ever been given. Once you understand the cash-flow at a weekly or even daily breakdown, the problem becomes smaller, the solutions more clear, and the sleepless nights fade away. If you sniff with arrogance at the accountant's insight, and refuse to become as one with the accountant, if not the actual accountant him/herself, prepare to repeat the phrase "cashflow crisis" more times than you ever thought possible.*

## Debt free growth is not forever

While the strategies outlined above, and some that you can probably envisage by now, take the sting out of cashflow management and support your efforts in debt-free growth, in my view they only delay the inevitable. At some point, you may need to either tone down your growth trajectory, because the pinch points are so dramatic, or seek other funding options to maintain your growth trajectory. If you project your business plan with a cashflow analysis and target your Exit

Strategy, you will see exactly what I mean. Eventually, like death and taxes, the bank or some other source of funding becomes a reality if your Exit Strategy extends far enough out into an aggressive-growth future.

This book does not discuss debt-leveraged growth. It's a perfectly viable strategy, and a very powerful one in its own right. I have simply not had the inclination to use it to achieve my goals.

## THREE TIPS

*Tip one*: Debt is a heavy burden for any company to bear, and – while it's not a sin to go into debt – it is a good decision to avoid it where possible. And it *is* possible if you predict your cashflow like a mathematician and watch it like a hawk.

*Tip two*: Consolidate before you grow. Make sure you save the profits until you have more than you need for your growth steps. But remember, if you grow in cells, you have a greater chance of growing in small steps.

*Tip three*: It is unlikely that you can keep growing indefinitely without going into debt, so understand that threshold well and, where possible, exit before you get there.

# CHAPTER 8
# PARTNERING

*Talent wins games,*
*but teamwork and intelligence wins championships*
*– Michael Jordan*

## Finding synergy

Consulting is a challenging industry because the threshold for entry is low. And competition is fierce. In your first few months, your first year or two years, you fight to climb above the many consultancies that compete for the smaller, bread-and-butter jobs. Despite your loftier ideals, the chances are that you will search for, and do, a significant amount of work that is less challenging or less creative than you would like.

You fight to recruit people, because you have no brand. There is a growth ceiling at three or four people in your company, and another – more substantial – growth ceiling at around twenty. You struggle to break through these ceilings, because they are not trivial or imaginary. There are many theories why these growth ceilings exist, and I suspect the real reason for their existence is a combination of these theories. But they exist, and they are a fact of your entrepreneurial consulting life.

The work can be hard and the hours long. Your enthusiasm and vision keeps you going, but there are many worries along the way. Growth is an uphill journey. It might be exhilarating, but it can be mentally exhausting. Keeping your mind fresh and energized is important; minimizing your worries is a strategic advantage. Worries shared with another are worries halved; just ask anyone in a healthy relationship.

At this point, there is an important observation to make. It takes only one person with vision to create a consulting empire. What is important is the vision and drive, the strategy and tactics, and their execution. Every single person has more than enough capacity to process these. The issue is not ability or capacity. The issue is time.

If you have the energy to work like a machine, and the resilience to power through days and weeks in single-minded determination, you can certainly build your enterprise by yourself. But if you seek work-life balance, if you have things to do on weekends that do not involve a lot of work, if you have a life partner or children for whom your time is precious, think about sharing the vision, the journey and the destination of your enterprise with another like-minded entrepreneur. If your preferred stress management technique is to avoid rather than process stress, and if you're inherently happier as part of a duet or small band than a solo artist, think about a partner.

I achieved my greatest successes because I had partners in entrepreneurship. Building a company by yourself is absolutely possible, but it can be a lonely ride. The burden is heavy, and shouldering it alone can be wearying after some time.

## Sharing the load

The most obvious reason to find a partner is, of course, to share the load. To ensure that you do not become a bottleneck to your own success because you get bogged down in the daily grind. To do this legitimately, you need to have similar skills. It helps no one if I'm weak at the financials and my partner is strong at financials, and yet we share the financial workload. My partner probably would (and certainly should) check my work, fix my mistakes and generally feel grumpy that I am not holding up my end.

Sharing the load works where the load to be shared is not rocket science. You're both pretty good at it (whatever the load is). You're both somewhat equally credentialed in your respective lines of expertise. On the administrative side, you dislike doing some things but you're capable of doing them, and it's the same for your partner.

Sharing the emotional load is important too. Building a business requires resilience, and not everyone is as stoic as the Terminator. It helps to have someone to vent with, to halve problems with, to provide perspectives that bolster your resilience when times are tough.

I think of "sharing the load" as a defensive strategy. One that divides labor and makes things a little bit easier. Like all defensive strategies, they are intended to stop you from sinking, and they do not necessarily turbo-charge your entrepreneurial engine.

Finding an "alike" partner is probably the easiest partnering exercise you can embark on. That is not to say that there are many of them, but if there is one, you recognize him or her quite quickly. They remind you of yourself. And like all things easy, it is not necessarily the best solution.

### *Tag team strengths*

*After some years of running his firm of 15 or so people alone, Peter brought in an equity partner, Carlos, and they began a growth program. Their firm specialized in environmental consulting for the mining industry. Much of their work involved site assessments, and most of the consultants, Peter and Carlos included spending days and sometimes two or three weeks at a time at remote sites around Australia and Asia.*

*Two years into the partnership, Peter's wife fell pregnant, but had a terrible pregnancy, beset by illness and concerns for the health of the growing baby. Peter, who had for many years advised at site on key strategies to gain approvals for some of the mines they consulted on, was unable to make many site trips. Carlos was able to take Peter's place, effectively doing a "double shift" for just under a year, covering critical workloads and ensuring that the firm did not lose ground in a very competitive environment.*

*Peter's wife had a healthy baby girl, and Peter resumed his site based activities some months after the birth. As he remarked later on, the business would have taken a significant hit if he, as the Principal, had been unable to advise clients on key decisions during that period. "Clients might sympathize as people," he said, "but client organizations don't have much sympathy. If you can't turn up for work, they'll go elsewhere."*

## Finding power in diversity

I believe that partners with complementary skills have a decided strategic advantage over partners with similar skills. Unless you are Superman or Superwoman, it is highly unlikely you will possess all of the skills required to start, build, consolidate, diversify and sell a consulting firm. It is unlikely that the same brain that envisions growth prospects is adept at watching your cashflow. It is unlikely the same personality that can sell new services to new clients is able to nurture and develop employees over a long period of time.

And if – despite its low likelihood – you *did* have all of these diverse skills, remember that (as we noted above) worries shared are worries halved, so a partner is still an asset. Some of the decisions you wrestle with are complex, with many variables, and an equal intellect with a shared vision helps stress test some of the decisions. So having a partner is still useful, although if you had all of these skills, you'd want an equal partner to equal your formidable skills, and then……. well, good luck finding *another* Superman or Superwoman!

## Avoiding key person risk

There is another, very compelling and basic reason, to think about partnering. There are three words that send a slight shiver down the spines of investors. *Key person risk*. With a single point of control comes a concentrated weakness. When you begin your enterprise, think about the next few years. What might happen to you? Could illness, or an accident, mar your next few years? Could changes to your personal circumstances – perhaps romance or children – appear in the next few years? Could you be called upon for family or friendship commitments that you need to honor? Now think about yourself as an investor. Would you invest in an enterprise that did not have these risks ameliorated to some extent? I would not.

### *Deliberate partnering*

*A partnership isn't a love-at-first-sight Hollywood fairytale match. It's something that needs a lot of work. Business is complex, and it is ruled by the mind, by insight backed by deep and thoughtful analysis, by deliberation and by consideration of options. Finding partners that will navigate this complexity to your satisfaction, and vice-versa from their perspective, can be a long process.*

*In my first partnership, a duo, it took nearly six months, with each of us successfully doing other things with our careers, to agree on a vision, an exit strategy, and a way to get there that inspired us both sufficiently to decisively commit. That was six months of coffees, beers, dinners and lunches – six months of good natured arguing, shooting down of each other's ideas and rebuilding them.*

*Of the six months, maybe three months were spent emailing each other spreadsheets and business plans, writing and rewriting. Neither of us was particularly pressed to do anything entrepreneurial. We both had successful careers and we had worked together in the past. We were halfway between acquaintances and true friends, and we both started with different ideas of what an enterprise might look like. We weren't hell bent on finding a way to work together. All we were doing was throwing an idea around and, like indulging in a hobby, crafting the idea until its shape and texture started to look to both of us like a work of art we might want to own together.*

## The dynamics of partnerships

Partnering is a tricky area. In Chapter One, I reminisced about my two consulting friends who pitched to me a partnership of sorts.

They proposed a collegiate, an informal banding together of sole-owner companies to find some kind of safety in numbers. There is nothing wrong with this model. It delivers benefits for the partners. But it is *not* a growth model. It is a support model. It is not a committed model; it is a membership model. It is a low-risk, moderate-benefit model. It is an opt-in, opt-out model.

A growth model works in partnership only when the architects of growth share a common vision and – equally importantly – are personally and professionally committed to this vision. Slightly lower on the hierarchy of needs for a growth model in partnership, but also critically important, is strong agreement on how specifically to achieve the vision.

There are many sporting analogies that successfully cross into the business world, and teamwork is one of them. Entrepreneurial consulting *could* work with larger teams at the helm, but consultants are egotistical creatures. The more people at the helm, the more difficult it is to reach decisions. Two at the helm might halve the worries. Three at the helm might share the burden more, but four at the helm probably creates more worries than it solves. For me, teamwork in entrepreneurial consulting is *not* like football – certainly not at the helm of the consulting enterprise. It's not a large team sport. The type of teamwork required is more likely to be like doubles tennis. It needs intuitive two-way communication, not a playmaker calling team strategy and tactics. Court presence, position and adaptability to each other's zones are all important. Trust is paramount; in the heat of play, if my partner says "go right", I go right instinctively. I don't ask "why?" We reserve that conversation for when the game is over. And that trust is reciprocated.

If you're not a sports fan, then the other analogy is a relationship. You and your partner – or partners – form a relationship and create a family. You trust each other's judgments, and you trust each other to discuss decisions before they are made. You argue, you settle, you commit to the agreed direction, and you don't fight in front of the kids. You face the world together but you debate in private on how you'll face it, striving to reach agreement, always committing to find agreement, and never acting unless agreement is reached.

I've just described relationship nirvana. But the chances of making a business partnership work at this level of commitment are quite good. For one, the relationship is less emotionally based than a romantic relationship, which bodes well for a rational partnership. For another, the partnership is not as highly dependent on (for example) split-second decisions on the tennis court, so the intensity of trust and intuitive co-dependence required is not as high as for championship doubles tennis players. It's actually easier to commit to the underlying partnership behaviors, provided you share the same vision and have a common view on how to achieve it.

Having said that, I have a great deal of respect for couples in a relationship that also run a successful growth enterprise. It's a rare thing for objective and subjective visions to be aligned, and for shared decision-making to work in both objective and subjective universes.

## The importance of governance

At the start of an enterprise in partnership, the G-word seems laughably bureaucratic, and sometimes even distasteful. But by the time you are ready to launch your exit strategy, it's one of your prime strengths. In the early days of your enterprise, it's forgivable to fly by the seat of your pants, but as your enterprise grows and matures, this is not enough. And governance starts at the Board, which is arguably where you and your partner(s) sit.

Where two partners are generally better than three when it comes to agreeing on decisions and moving quickly (if you are both aligned), a two-partner board can become paralyzed when there is a difference of opinion on something important. If there is a 50-50 partnership with equivalent voting rights, the paralysis can become very serious indeed. Governance processes that skirt deadlock situations are essential as you grow.

I think of this as a bit of a pre-nuptial agreement about how you agree, and how you agree to disagree. It may be as simple as having another Board member or members executive and non-executive – distribution of voting rights, agreement on a Chairperson's casting vote, or any number of pre-determined deadlock-breakers. Or it may be as complex as agreed processes for decision-making on material aspects of your enterprise. Whatever you do, agree on one thing at the start. Agree that you *will* disagree on things, and you do not want that disagreement to become constraining or debilitating to your enterprise.

## Partnerships, diversity and alignment internally

Every partnership is different. Your own role in every partnership is different. If you approach partnerships with a cookie-cutter approach, you risk every partnership you initiate. Bespoke is the key.

While finding common ground in the big things (vision, strategy, tactics) is essential, common ground in the small things (stationery, office color schemes, wording of internal memos) is also important.

It is important enough to avoid glossing over. If your vision, strategy and tactics are the bricks in your enterprise, the small things are the mortar.

It is too easy, at the start of the enterprise, to get carried away by the audacity of your vision and to trivialize the little things as 'administrative distractions'. Discord on those little things can add up, slowly and insidiously. Discord is very easy for others to intuit. Your staff sense it, without knowing what they are sensing, other than that it isn't positive. Strategies for dealing with discord between partners (and discord is all but inevitable) are essential to developing your enterprise and to keeping your staff focused and productive. The kids mustn't see their parents fighting.

While partnering with someone might logically compel you to divide up your labor – "you do this and I'll do that" – the reality is that equal partners can feel the need to have an equal say in everything, and to be equally involved in everything. Or at least in things that they feel like being involved in. This can be inefficient and counterproductive. But in order to determine what the most sensible division of labor is, you need to do several things. The first is that you need to be clear on all the tasks that need to be done. This is the easy part. The second is that you need to recognize and be honest about each other's strengths and weaknesses. This is much harder, because we all have our blind spots about the things that we are not so good at. And some of these blind spots can be borderline delusional.

The third part, which is also not so easy, is that you agree to divide up the work according to your strengths, and you agree on the collaboration and decision-making processes that will ensure you remain partners and arrive at agreement on the important issues. This might result in an *I'll lead on this and you lead on that* agreement. Then there is a fourth part. When you divide up the tasks that need to be carried out, you may realize that there is a set of tasks that neither of you is particularly strong at, and worse, some tasks that neither of you want to do. Like the remainder on a long division operation in arithmetic, you look at the leftover bit with a vague sense of dissatisfaction. And, like true partners, you agree on dividing up the crap (and how you'll support each other's weaknesses in dealing with the crap).

## Partners to the outside world

One of the more important labor division activities in consulting is client stewardship. When you start the enterprise, and indeed until you exit, the partners are the figureheads. In the eyes of all clients, you and your partner(s) are the head honchos, the royalty of your organization. So you each want to be accessible to your clients. If clients are accessing the royalty of your enterprise, they feel important. But clients are people too, and these relationships are as much about the personal connections as they are about the work you do. Matching you to the right clients, and you partner(s) to the right clients is essential. And the four parts of labor division apply equally to this aspect too. What is the list of clients? Which ones are you really good with/which ones do you get along with? Which ones am I good with/which ones do I get along with? There are some left over; how do we divide them up?

My general philosophy has always been that you, the principal of your enterprise, needs to have lots of face time with your clients while your employees run the projects. This doesn't mean you are merely a liaison officer. It means you are across the strategy of the consulting assignments, you add value to the assignments, you troubleshoot, you soothe the client in difficult times, you find and enact solutions when there appear to be none, and above all you get the best out of your employees for your clients.

When there are two or more of you – partners – there is an added social complexity. You want your clients to feel like they have at least ceremonial access to *all* of the royalty of your enterprise, not just one member of royalty. I've always found this aspect of partnerships to be hugely value-adding. If you are a potent partnership, a team (as opposed to a pairing or collection of individuals), your true and unique value is in your collusion. Recognizing this and leveraging it can substantially lift your business development activities. Bear in mind that I am not talking about Batman-and-Robin partnerships, but something more like Batman-and-Superman partnerships.

I've genuinely lost count of the number of times, during our ceremonial discussions with clients (perhaps once every three or six months, perhaps over lunch or dinner) when two partners working together doubled, tripled or quadrupled the value of a consulting assignment by increasing the scope of the assignment or elevating the scope of the assignment. The diversity of perspective, powerfully aligned between two or more partners, can take problem-solving to a higher level, and when clients recognize that, the chemistry you bring as partners becomes a highly sought-after commodity. Think of the successes of the buddy-cop movies or the comedy duos or the musical collaborations that have dotted the entertainment landscape. The magic lay in the interaction of the partners more than it lay in the individual appeal of each partner. These are the great, transcending partnerships that accelerate growth and prosperity, the teamwork that can transform a successful enterprise into a dynamic market-raider.

## Partnerships: there is no right model

Over the years I have met with both parties of several successful two-partner ventures. What has struck me is that the personalities that developed and grew successful ventures were very different from each other. I've labeled some of the more remarkable partnerships I've seen, with such clichés as Good Cop/Bad Cop, Nerd/Jock, Ice Queen/Mother Theresa and Brain/Brawn. Diversity at the helm can be very powerful. When leveraged well, only the best decisions make it through. Poor or average choices fall by the wayside. Good ideas, following principles of Darwinism, adapt to become better and better as they are bounced between different partners until their chance of survival are optimized. Bad ideas become extinct. This is an organizational strength that should not be underestimated. It has its dark side – the inability to make timely decisions – but if the dark side is avoided it's a formidable strategic advantage. We all have our strengths and weaknesses, our blind spots and our realms of clarity. It is important to cover for weaknesses with governance and with respectful debate, and to harness the strengths needed to gain maximum wattage.

And that, in a nutshell, should be your underlying partnership strategy. Undoubtedly, a good partnership will allow you to share the load and potentially bring more work-life balance to your life at the helm of your enterprise. But a great partnership will multiply the intrinsic value of your enterprise by harvesting the energy created by your interaction, your collusion, your chemistry and your teamwork. And allow you to achieve things greater than the sum of each of you could achieve.

## THREE TIPS

*Tip one*: Spend a great deal of time in contemplation about your part-ner(s) before you choose him or her or them. You need to be in tune almost at the level of your business DNA.

*Tip two*: Don't set foot in a partnership without a pre-nuptial; a clear agreement on how decisions will be made. Don't allow a deadlock scenario to develop at the Board; it will cripple you if it happens, particularly if there are only two of you. Use non-executive di-rectors and casting votes to prevent your organization from paralyzing from within.

*Tip three*: It may sound obvious, but make sure you get along with your partner as a person. If you're at ease with each other, it multiplies your chances that your journey will be fun.

# CHAPTER 9
# STUMBLING

*I like to make my own mistakes*
*– Mikhail Baryshnikov*

## Flawless execution

Show me an entrepreneur who claims to have defined and executed strategy perfectly, and I'll show you a liar. I spent a lot of time looking for mistakes others had made, and then a lot of time finding ways to avoid making them. Mostly, I was successful in avoiding them. But then I made my own unique mistakes, and I'm sure those mistakes numbered the same as the average entrepreneur.

The lesson I learned was this. You are going to stumble. It is a fact, a statistical reality you can't avoid. By all means strive to avoid it (you'd be foolish not to), but accept that mistakes will be made. Your mindset is important here. How you sense the mistake early, how you recover and how you learn are three crucial pillars of this mindset.

To list the mistakes you shouldn't make would fill a book by itself. And to be fair, recounting the mistakes of others doesn't add a lot of value. For a start, you can find out about them yourself. Secondly, I didn't learn anything substantial from mistakes I didn't make, so I have nothing to pass on to you. So I will limit this chapter to mistakes I made, and learnt from.

## Growing too fast

The problem with growing too fast is that self-sustaining funding becomes an interesting but largely abstract concept. And while growing too fast might sound like a problem you'd be glad to have, it can lead to a cashflow disaster and insolvency. When you're chasing growth, it's difficult to recognize too much growth, and it's hard to find the discipline to forcibly slow down your growth, and your ego can get in the way of making sensible decisions even if your ability to recognize and your discipline to act on it are both good.

Seeing this mistake early requires you to peer intensely into the mirror of your cashflow analysis, and through the window of your sales growth. Remember, you have to hire and pay people to produce the work to give the client and to get paid for it. So when you haul in contract after contract, and every month you are selling considerably more than the month before, and the office echoes with the sound of heartily-slapped high fives, your wages crank up as you put on more people to make your fees to salary ratio hit that sweet spot. You eat into your cash reserves quickly while you wait for the work to be done and the achingly slow clients to pay up. This Twilight Zone of high productivity and no revenue is your Work in Progress. All organizations have to deal with this to some extent. They have to finance the activities of producing something until they are able to realize the revenues that the production brings.

The simplest solution is to just say no. But this is easier said than done. In a feast-to-famine industry, saying no is taboo. I've said no.

Clients then questioned our capacity to do larger jobs, and came to us more cautiously in the future. So I actually regretted saying no.

A more measured solution is to not chase as many projects. If you're being phenomenally successful with your pitches, then pitch fewer proposals. This worked better for me.

Later on, as I became bolder, I tried telling clients who offered us projects that I could certainly undertake them as long as they could pay a commencement installment of the fee. Typically I'd ask for 20-25% of the project fee up front. This put cash in our coffers early, giving us the cushion needed to put on staff for new projects. This was a somewhat less successful tactic than not chasing projects, as many clients had procurement policies that did not allow for pre-payment of services (although they did have such policies for the partial pre-payment of capital equipment (such as machinery) and capital works (such as construction). So the tactic did, on occasion, backfire and clients then questioned our ability to do larger jobs. But it worked more often than not.

## Hiring the HR manager

There comes a point in your growth where it dawns on you that, no matter how good you are at attracting and retaining people, you don't have the time to do this. There comes a time when you need people systems so that you can treat people fairly and methodically, even though you don't really know all their names. There comes a time when you can't keep up with the constantly changing labor laws and regulations that you, as a Director, need to abide by. This is when you decide you need a Human Resources manager.

What I didn't realize, when I first took this step, was that I was about to introduce a significant change to the way my employees viewed their relationship with the company. Previously they had direct access to the owner(s), who made all the people decisions in what felt like a family business. Now a complete stranger was about to make those decisions.

Realizing the magnitude of the change that will be perceived by your people will, hopefully, make you much more careful about how you bring in a Human Resources manager than I was.

It is a mistake to assume that HR managers get your culture. Like any other employee, they come neatly packaged with their previous experiences and systems. The HR manager from a larger organization might have been used to less 'personal' processes, and a more clinically objective approach than you've nurtured. The impact on morale can be huge.

Worse, the HR manager can introduce politics into the organization, at a scale that you might not believe possible. If you don't believe me, consider this. The HR manager is one of the most powerful and influential people in your organization because he or she knows as much as anyone knows about all of your people, how they are rewarded, and what their strengths and weaknesses are. If knowledge is power, the HR manager is a very powerful individual indeed. And the wrong person in that role can turn that power into a deeply disruptive influence, especially in a consulting organization, where your main asset is your people.

The nightmare does not end there. HR managers know the rights of employees, and they know their own rights very well. If you hire your HR manager poorly, once you realize your mistake, getting rid of that person is a long and painful process.

Of course, a good HR person is a real asset to your organization. The point I'm making is that choosing poorly is a large and costly mistake. It's costly from a morale perspective, and financially costly because of the loss of productivity and the legal ramifications of trying to remove the HR manager.

The easy answer is, of course, to choose wisely. It is also prudent to carefully craft the employment contract to include appropriate probationary periods and processes, and legally acceptable ways to terminate the employment.

But I'd be inclined to also consider the option of outsourcing HR systems functions and keeping the 'relations' function – the part that involved nurturing your people – in your scope of activity. Why? Because in consulting, your people are truly your greatest asset. It isn't rhetoric, you actually have no other asset. And if you only have one asset to look after, to whom should you entrust it?

## Growing too far

We discussed earlier in this chapter about growing too fast, of winning more work than your cash reserves can support during Work in Progress. Geographical growth is another type of growth that can prove to be a costly mistake if not managed well.

Geographical growth can be advantageous as it allows you to tap into new markets. And it should be a legitimate part of your strategy. But while geographical growth can be enticing it comes with risk. The risk arises because your growth happens *over there*. Setting up over there requires a fair bit of your financial reserves. Every new office is like a new capital venture, and it impacts on your bank account. And – perhaps even more importantly – if you're *over there* managing that growth, you're not *over here* managing your foundation operation. Sun Tzu, the great military tactician, pointed out that you should conquer new lands only after your existing constituency is stable.

One of my early mistakes was to ambitiously grow both nationally and internationally. I had a perfectly feasible, but slightly irrational, "four continents in four years" goal. It wasn't that I was aiming for a one-person office in each of four continents. No, I wanted the flagship office, my first office, replicated to a similar scale in three other continents.

This was actually achieved successfully – but at what cost? Firstly, while our revenues skyrocketed, our profitability diminished because not every office was a star performer. Secondly, every office startup required capital, and that capital took one to two years to replenish. So opening four offices in four years left us with diminished cash reserves. Thirdly, for four years, I spent most of my time on long haul flights. Whilst being ridiculously expensive, it also made me very tired and I lost control of work-life balance. Fourthly, I started losing the personal contact I had with my staff, as there were simply not enough hours in any given year to nurture the number of people in the different countries who were instrumental in the success of the firm.

The net result of this was that 'growing too far' resulted in a measurably (but not drastically) lower return on capital overall, tangibly less effective grooming of the management team that would take over at exit, and a loss of work-life balance that I could not get back. The experience taught me never again to underestimate the challenge of geographical growth, it taught me to go deliberately slow when expanding to other countries, and it is a constant reminder that when you create ego-driven goals like "four continents in four years", you must critically and objectively question yourself.

## Hire slowly, fire quickly, equity in inches

Cliched though it is, this is a fine adage to live by. It is also a difficult adage to live by when you are growth oriented and time is ticking as you journey toward your exit strategy. I would dearly like to say that I have always hired wisely, but the most honest thing I can say is that every year I hired more wisely than the previous.

No matter how good your interviewing techniques are, how sophisticated the interview panels are, and how cleverly you use psychometric evaluations, you *will* hire duds. OK, you will hire fewer duds because you've been quite strategic, but you will hire them nonetheless.

It takes me anywhere between six months and two years to rectify the mistake of hiring a dud. I used to think this was either really myopic or really slow of me, but over time I realized that most people (including me) take six to twenty-four months to realize, and come to terms with the realization, that they have hired poorly. The 'honeymoon period' lasts three to six months. The denial period lasts six to twelve months. The extraction period can be six to twelve months. It all adds up.

A classic 'honeymoon' mistake is to grant equity too early. You want people enthused, you feel good about the gun General Manager you have just hired, and the process of negotiation takes you to equity discussions.

After my first mistake, I realized there are three key elements to minimizing the risk of these mistakes recurring. The first is to set probationary periods with key performance indicators (KPIs), and preferably have probationary periods that are much longer than the 'honeymoon period'. The second is to write your employment contracts carefully so that you can legally terminate employment decisively if the KPIs are not met. And the third is to drip feed equity over a number of years.

The mistake of not doing these things well extends in a halo effect well past you and the dud employee. The longer you hold onto a dud employee, the more demoralizing it is for your star employees. They know stars and duds when they see them, and it is very difficult to breed a winning culture if your systems are too weak to eject poor employees effectively and efficiently.

## Governance before you need it

When you first start up your enterprise, you might make all the decisions. Why? Mostly because you can. And partly because there isn't anyone else to make them.

When you first start up a partnership, there is someone else to make them, but if you're a small enough enterprise it doesn't take much to make collaborative decisions.

Later on in your enterprise, two things happen. There are other people who make decisions on your behalf, and in a partnership it becomes more and more difficult to collaborate on all key decisions. In those situations, it really is only a matter of time before someone makes a decision that you not only disagree with, but it impacts on the long term prosperity of the organization.

Knowing this – that it is only a matter of time before this happens – should give you the foresight to put in governance mechanisms before you reach that point. If you're like me, you'll wait until your first significant mis-step before you scramble to put in well-thought out governance processes into your organization.

It's quite easy to identify which business decisions require governance. They are the decisions that matter to you, the owner(s) and directors, the ones you don't want to get wrong. They are also the ones that you want to navigate disagreements on, if you have partners. It's as simple as making a list of the key decisions that require governance, and then writing down the steps for each one that give you, the owner(s), comfort that rash or damaging decisions are unlikely to be made.

The main learning is that, even if it seems like a waste of time and effort, put in governance well before you need it. You will avoid many poor and costly decisions, and you will sleep better at night knowing they are there.

## Hire the best PA you can

PA's everywhere will cheer at this section. I know it sounds trivial, and almost narcissistic, but this is one of the best decisions you can make, and one of the most irritating if you get it wrong. A loyal and diligent PA will make your entrepreneurial life much easier than an average PA will. Here's why.

Building and running your own company can be an all-consuming activity. Because it is your baby, you tend to give it a lot of attention. If you're like me, and others concur, you actually give it more attention than you give yourself.

Just like the airline emergency instructions that encourage you to put your own oxygen mask on before attending to others, a good PA will ensure that you keep yourself physically, mentally and emotionally armed to look after your people and your company. I have had a few colleagues look at me sideways at this mothering, nurturing picture I paint of a good PA, but I – and many others I know – stand by this. Certainly, you need your PA to do the usual things with skill and finesse: organize your diary, shield you from unwanted trivia, ensure your travel plans go without a hitch, bring you financial reports, remind you of others' birthdays and significant events, and hunt down General Managers that are missing in action. Finding a PA that does all these things well is not that hard. Finding a PA who watches you work and cares enough to do the myriad, fine-tuning, invisible things in the background to make you more effective and efficient is gold.

If you are diligent (and lucky) enough to find a PA who does this, treat him or her well. No matter how many able and loyal General Managers you have, your PA will be your valued lieutenant.

The PAs that cancel your meetings the morning after a long trip, and sternly order you to sleep in, go for a swim, have a leisurely breakfast and come in ready to be effective, are the ones you want. The ones that come in to your office, shut the door, sit down and ask "OK, what's bothering you?" are the ones you want. The ones who cry when you announce your exit plans; the ones you want to take with you to your next role are the ones you want. Don't settle for anything less.

CHAPTER 10

# EXIT

*I been a long time leaving but I'm going to be a long time gone*
*– Willie Nelson*

## Initiating the exit

If we were being philosophical, we would say that you had initiated your exit back at the point when you had conceived of your plan to create a consulting organization. However, the practical kick-off point of initiating an exit is when you begin signaling your intentions externally. I like to think of it as preparing to leave the party. You don't skulk away or make a beeline for the exit. That's just rude, and people notice you're gone anyway. You circulate, purposefully, in a general locus towards your hat and coat, but letting your friends and hosts know that you are thinking of going home. Hopefully they all say "oh no, but it's still early! Stick around, have some more shiraz!" But you continue, politely and relentlessly, towards the door.

It is important, and I can't stress enough how important it is for operational continuity and morale, that your exit is not sprung as some last-minute surprise on your staff. You risk abandonment issues, loss of trust, general consternation and a deep organizational worry that you are leaving a scuttled ship. From a practical perspective, you risk a greater staff turnover and loss of productivity, both of which stick out like a sore thumb to a prospective buyer.

There is no more important time for finesse than when you initiate the exit. There are three things I aim for, in this sequence: first, your staff should know that that time has come, but it will be a leisurely process. You're not running away. Second, prospective buyers should know that you have an intention, but not an imperative, to sell. And third, your clients should know that you're considering a long and overdue break from being captain of the ship.

It's not always possible to program your exit this way. Other factors, such as ill health, can lead to a rushed exit. But most of the time you can initiate the exit early, with plenty of cues and direct signals, to underpin a smooth transition.

You need to have your house in order before initiating the exit, of course. There are just three things to watch for. One, responsibility and accountability should have devolved to others a while ago, to the point where your overt leadership presence is now little more than a happy memory, and (hopefully while valued) is not a necessity anymore. Two, your company's performance should be on year three, four or five of an upward trend. And three, your books – your financial administration – should be in perfectly balanced, transparent order. And this should, of course, include some valuation calculations, as we discussed back in Chapter 2. When these three are lined up, you can begin your conversations; the ones that start with "we've been talking about this for a long time now, and I guess now is as good a time as any to start thinking about….." If you've done things right, you'll have a great feeling when you have those conversations, and a sense of building excitement.

## Your people

You would need to be a borderline sociopath to not feel a sense of impending loss when you're embarking on a sale process. Despite the excitement of almost realizing your vision for exit – fulfilling your ultimate reason for starting this enterprise – you've grown your own firm from scratch. You've hired many of the people yourself, choosing carefully, nurturing, passing on what you can, watching them make their own way in their professional lives, giving them a stake in your venture. You've created a family. Some individuals you like, some not so much, but the collective, the family, is something you've invested your soul into.

But people, as they say, are funny types. Some are fine, almost neutral, with your impending departure. They are more concerned about who's taking over and what it means for them. It would be great if all of your staff were like this, but alas no. A surprising number of your staff will feel like children about to be abandoned. They will be uncertain, resentful even, that you're cashing out. What happened to all that "we are one" rhetoric you used to preach, they might ask. What happened to solidarity? You were scheming all along to sell up and move on?

If you're a pragmatist, none of this matters as long as they continue to be effective and productive hunters, farmers, creatives and closers. If you like people, and you want this effectiveness and productivity to be assured, you'll invest heavily in speaking with your employees, one on one and in groups, to bring them along with you in the sale process. Don't be in so much of a hurry to leave that you neglect your people. It shows. It erodes value.

*Growing and Selling a Successful Consulting Firm*

### The pain of parting

*Jim, an elder statesman who had made a wildly successful exit a decade or more before I had started thinking about an enterprise, recalled to me once how he'd initiated his exit from a spectacularly successful sustainability firm. The signals, he said, had been loud and clear for almost two years. He had been taking more skiing trips, and he had always come back remarking that he could do skiing trips all year. He had started taking Wednesday afternoons off for golf and turning up politely late on Monday mornings. His presence at Board meetings was benign, he said. "I vaguely disagreed with half the decisions made, but they were trivial disagreements, ones that did not materially affect company culture or value, and it was important that the leadership of the company made decisions that were not heavily influenced by me."*

*Nonetheless, he recalled, his conversations were universally met with anguish by his staff. "But you're too young to retire!" was the most common protest he received.*

*Despite all that he'd done to signal his intentions, his staff went into a phase that he called "pre-mourning". Jim's observation was this. In a happy culture, self-induced change can be menacing. Why change if all is good? Or, more pointedly, things are perfect now, any change can only be for the worse. Jim's experience was, I thought, the perfect manifestation of the two-edged sword of elegant exits. I asked him how he handled it. "I spent a lot of the next eight or nine months circulating and talking, checking in on projects, showing people that I was still interested, I still cared, even if it was time for a change for me," he said. "And I told them their future was in their hands, not mine."*

## The buyers

Play the field. When you are ready to sell, you should have already identified your potential suitors, and you should have already have had many courtship meetings during which you've signaled that you'll probably sell in the not-too-distant future. You want as many buyers interested as possible. The price goes up, and the deal gets done quicker. If you only have one buyer, be prepared for a more laborious deal and be prepared to settle for a lower price if you really want out.

It's hard to know what to expect when engaging with a buyer. At the heart of it all, it's a negotiation of course. You want the highest price, they want the lowest. There are other things you want – stability for your staff, a sense of continuity, the safe handover of a brand, and client stewardship. They want stability too, but they will want change. Systems might change to their systems. Roles in your company might change to roles that complement existing structures they have. Some buyers will approach the purchase with finesse, while others might be clumsier. None of these are things you can control, although your advice will be mostly welcomed by an astute buyer. No-one wants to spook the horse they are about to ride, and you – the leader – knows the horse best.

Hostile buys in consulting are rare, but possible. A sense of urgency on the buyer's part can contribute to this. The timing of a large contract, for example, can influence how a buyer approaches you. If a buyer wants the sale complete before the profits from the large contract start come in, things can get heated. In a negotiating sense this can work to your advantage, but the temperature in the kitchen can be more intense than you'd planned for.

Whether amicable or hostile (and in my direct experience, as well as from the stories of others, most deals are on the amicable side of average) I think there is one thing to bear in mind. You are still the captain of your ship, and you should shield your charges from any turbulence that the sale process brings. If you have shared the equity around well, your sale team includes the key people in your organization. They are part of the negotiation, which can take the pressure off you, but also increase the complexity of the negotiation process. But unless you are a minority shareholder, the negotiation is largely about financing you to leave for a different life. So you are a key stakeholder.

Buyers baulk when you display reluctance at their reasonable requests, or are sluggish in meeting their requests. Accounts should be produced promptly. Interviews with key personnel should be scheduled quickly and with minimum fuss. Treat the sale like an important project and prioritize it. Anticipate what will be asked for (they will be much the same as the things you would ask for if buying a firm like yours!), and have these things ready before you initiate the exit. The sale process can move very quickly if you're ready. No buyer wants to make an offer, then have another buyer make a better counter offer. A bidding war does not suit a buyer; it suits you the seller. So the two rules here are to court as many buyers as you can, and to have everything ready before you initiate.

## Your clients

Of the three groups of people we consider in this chapter, clients seem to be the least flustered by a sale process. You don't want them to find out from someone else, of course, but nonetheless it can seem pretty surreal when you gently spring your 'big news' on them over lunch and they are more interested in telling you how much they like the great facelift the restaurant had since last year.

But of course, that makes sense. If you've done your job well, executed strategy well, you're the person they occasionally have lunch with, the person who asks for frank feedback and then (hopefully) does something subtle to achieve some kind of continuous improvement in service. Hell, the only thing they associate you with is lunches and philosophical chats, maybe some strategy. You're no good to talk detail with; you lost that ability with them a long time ago.

Still, the reassurance from you that nothing changes, delivery of assignments is paramount and service is second to nothing is essential. Expected, and essential. If you weren't doing the rounds and satisfying this simple hygiene protocol, there would be something wrong, something fishy.

The exit conversations with clients are, in my experience, the most relaxing of all. They ask if you'll consult back to them. You say (regretfully) that this will not happen for a while because you will not compete with your old organization (and your buyer will probably insist on this in the sale contract anyway). Some of them will tell you of a role in their organization, or offer you a job. If you do it right, you'll walk away warm and fuzzy, and with a deep sense of wellbeing, from the exit conversations with clients.

## The expense of a sale

Selling a company isn't a cheap activity. Just getting your books in order, audited and transparent, laid out for sale rather than to appease the tax-man, costs you. Diverting key people – especially those with equity – from assignments so that they can be part of the sale process is expensive. And we haven't even started talking about the lawyers and their fees.

Much of the expense of a sale (for you as well as the buyer) can be reduced if you and the buyer work together to agree the terms. Starting with a Memorandum of Understanding, you can move seamlessly into articulating in plain English what each of you agrees to. Together you can write a simple but thorough contract if you are willing to spend the time trying. Then hand this over to the lawyers, who will find Machiavellian ways each of you can screw the other, and then proceed to write convoluted clauses that neutralize the nefarious schemes they've dreamed up. It will feel like they are jousting on your behalf. All you can do is shake your head and laugh. But regardless, agreeing the terms of your contract before involving lawyers will save both time and money, on both sides.

It's important that billable work continues unabated through the months of executing a sale, and no matter how convenient it may seem, try to avoid working through the sale process in your company offices. There are many reasons to do things in the office – the books are easier to go through, interviews are much easier to conduct, clarifications are much easier to make. There is just one outstanding reason not to do this. It distracts your staff. Billable hours go down. You may think that locking the Boardroom and confining all activity to that chamber will stop the distraction, but the entire company knows that wheeling and dealing is being carried out in that room, and it dominates conversations. Walk out of the Boardroom looking frustrated or harassed, and the rumor mill spins into overdrive. It simply isn't worth it. Let your enterprise do what it's been bred to do, while you execute your exit strategy from someone else's offices – your buyer's, your accountant's, or a leased office space down the road.

## The time it takes

This is probably one of the most frequently asked questions regarding a sale. How long does it take from initiation to completion? The answer, in true consultant's fashion, is "it depends". It depends on how keen the buyer is. It depends on how flexible you, and your other shareholders, are on the sale price. It depends on how well you've prepared. It depends on whether the organization continues to perform smoothly while negotiations proceed. If pressed, my answer is three to nine months, with exceptions well in excess of nine months if things go awry.

The time is, inevitably, one of heightened stress. Because you have expectations, ones that you created back when you started your enterprise. Because the buyer asks for increasing levels of detail, some that you hadn't thought they'd be interested in. Because your staff start asking, like kids in the back seat of the car, "are we there yet?" It's important to make time for clear thinking and good decisions during this period, and it's important to stay fit and healthy, well fed and well rested.

And suddenly, before you know it, the end is there. Everyone is ready to sign. There are lots of papers to sign and countersign in the final session. Lawyers drone on, papers pass from the buyer to you, from you to the buyer, your pen gets a workout, there are lots of handshakes. Hopefully everyone is smiling, because you have created a valuable asset, the buyer is a proud new owner of this asset, and you've realized its value. Your bank account looks like it's been hit by an internet error in your favor, and you're now faced with the next phase of your future. You're all fueled up and ready to go.

### Exit stress

*Many entrepreneurs who have sold willingly have remarked that the stress they endured during the sale process seemed to have been more than it should have been. Horst, a consummate entrepreneur who executed his sale process over a period of six months, disappeared off the face of the earth to recuperate for nearly a year. I think he was surfing remote beaches around south east Asia and the Pacific. When he returned, I asked him how the process went.*

*"It was actually very straightforward," he mused. "I think most of the stress was self-generated. I agonized about giving away five percent here or there. In fact, I took every negotiation point as a slight on the company value…. The company I valued, my baby."*

*"Isn't five percent worth fighting for?" I asked, already knowing the answer.*

*"Well, yes and no. On principle. And in practice. In hindsight though, a five percent move in the valuation doesn't reduce my future options by five percent. It doesn't dent my plans at all. So yes, negotiate hard, but not to the point where you lose perspective and take things personally. You're about to become independently wealthy, plus or minus five percent, and if you can avoid the need to de-stress for a year as a result of that happy outcome, you probably should."*

## What's on the other side?

People are inquisitive about what happens to you after you sell your successful consulting firm. It's a loaded question. You do something you're passionate about, and it pervades your working life; and possibly even life outside work. You grow the firm, and you grow people, and it feels like a family. It's successful and you want to sell at the height of success, which is a bit like leaving the Grand Prix while you're a lap in front. You go from being the hero in your own comic book to just another reader. I understand very well why people stay too long. It requires discipline to exit.

And yes, there is a sense of loss on exit. A large part of your life disappears. There's relief, and there's a void to fill. I'm sure different people feel a different pang of loss, but the successful entrepreneurs I've talked to about selling their consulting firm say the same thing. It's bittersweet. But then, all successful conclusions are. It's a chapter closing, and another one opening. You just have to pick up your pen and start writing the new chapter, and occasionally re-read the old one for pleasure.

I often point out that, even though I insist first on an exit strategy, the beauty of your adventure is the journey. The sale is your period, or exclamation point (if you're lucky!) but the journey is your sentence, or your proverb.

And that, my friend, is all I have to offer. If I have filled you with enthusiasm and armed you better for your enterprise, then I am glad and I wish you well. If you have been entertained, but not yet energized to grow and sell your own successful enterprise, then rest assured, there is no hurry. When the time is right, it will feel right; do it when you're ready. It's not hard – in fact, as a rocket scientist friend of mine once said, "It's not rocket science".

## ABOUT RAJ ASEERVATHAM

Raj Aseervatham is an untalented engineer who turned an unpromising engineering career in mining into something more fulfilling – advising corporations on their ethics, integrity, governance practices, societal performance, transparency and their reputations. He has worked for over twenty-five years in large industry, in government and in global consulting, in many countries and on most continents on the planet. He has a PhD in engineering, an MBA, is a Fellow of the Institution of Engineers Australia and a Graduate of the Australian Institute of Company Directors.

When he's not encouraging senior corporate executives to do the right thing and showing them how, he watches his three children grow alarmingly quickly and writes to relax.

www.ingramcontent.com/pod-product-compliance
Lightning Source LLC
Chambersburg PA
CBHW050124210326
41519CB00015BA/4090